Legal information

© 2023
Author and Editor: M.Eng. Johannes Wild
A94689H39927F
Email: 3dtech@gmx.de

The complete imprint of the book can be found on the last pages!

This work is protected by copyright

Preface (Important Information about the Book!)

How to use this book and what you can expect from it

Thank you very much for choosing this book!

Probably everyone knows that Microsoft Excel is a powerful spreadsheet program. But most people only know the basic functions and cannot use the hidden treasures in Excel. This misery is over now. In this book, you will learn how to make full use of Excel's top functions. This book equips you with the most important tools in your daily struggle with the flood of data and information that we are exposed to in our private and professional lives today.

Bring order to your tables and shine with sophisticated Excel knowledge. Not only will you impress your superiors, but you will also have helpful tools at your fingertips in your private life. For the administration of personal property, real estate, planning birthday parties and much more.

To provide a clear introduction at all levels, the book is divided into "Basic" and "Expert" topics within the chapters. The "Basic" sections explain basic functions that provide everyday help. In the "Expert" chapters, we go a little deeper into the subject and learn advanced functions for the corresponding topic. Each chapter contains theoretical instructions (illustrated & step by step) as well as many practical examples.

The font color of the chapter headings reflects the difficulty level, "Basic" or "Expert". As a beginner, you should read all chapters from the beginning, especially chapters with green writing ("Basic"). Chapters with violet font color are interesting for beginners as well as for advanced users. And as an advanced Excel user, you can skip green chapters and start immediately with the blue chapters ("Expert").

Of course, this is only a classification according to the author's feeling. You have to find out for yourself what level you are at in Excel. So please take this classification only as a recommendation.

The "Ribbon", which will be mentioned frequently, can be found in Excel at the top, just below the green bar, including well-known functions such as "Save", "Undo", etc.

This book is suitable for Microsoft Excel 2010, 2013, 2016 & 2019 as well as Microsoft Office 365. The information in this book was created using Excel from Microsoft Office 365, so some features of the Excel versions may differ from earlier versions (especially 2010 & 2013). This also applies to design elements. Don't let it throw you off track. In the end, you will certainly learn many great functions!

Try to actively practice the examples and theoretical considerations in Excel, rather than just reading the book. This is essential to internalize the functions as you know for sure: Only practice makes perfect!

Let's get started!

Table of Contents

1 Excel Interface & Settings

At the beginning, you will get a first overview of Excel's user interface and the basic functions & settings. In this section we will discuss very basic things, i.e., if you have already used Excel a few times, you can skip **chapter 1.1**. However, you should follow the recommended settings in **chapter 1.2.**

1.1 Excel Interface & Important Sections

We start with the red framed area in *Fig. 1*, where you can navigate through the ribbon. If some sections are not displayed in the ribbon, you have to activate them first, as explained in Chapter **1.2**. The section "Home" includes basic functions.

In the orange framed area you will find the cell "name box". By default, this is specified with an alphanumeric reference (A1, B2,…). However, you can also name the cell as you wish. To do this, select the orange-framed cell field and write the name, then confirm with "Enter". Note that you must now use the new name for each reference to this cell.

The area framed in blue is used to enter a function (but normal text or numbers can also be entered). For a selection and description of possible functions, click on the small f_x symbol.

In the green framed section in the lower area, you will find the possibility to add and manage further worksheets. In the yellow area you can scale the display (zoom) and choose between "normal display", "page layout" or "page break view". Just try out the different display options!

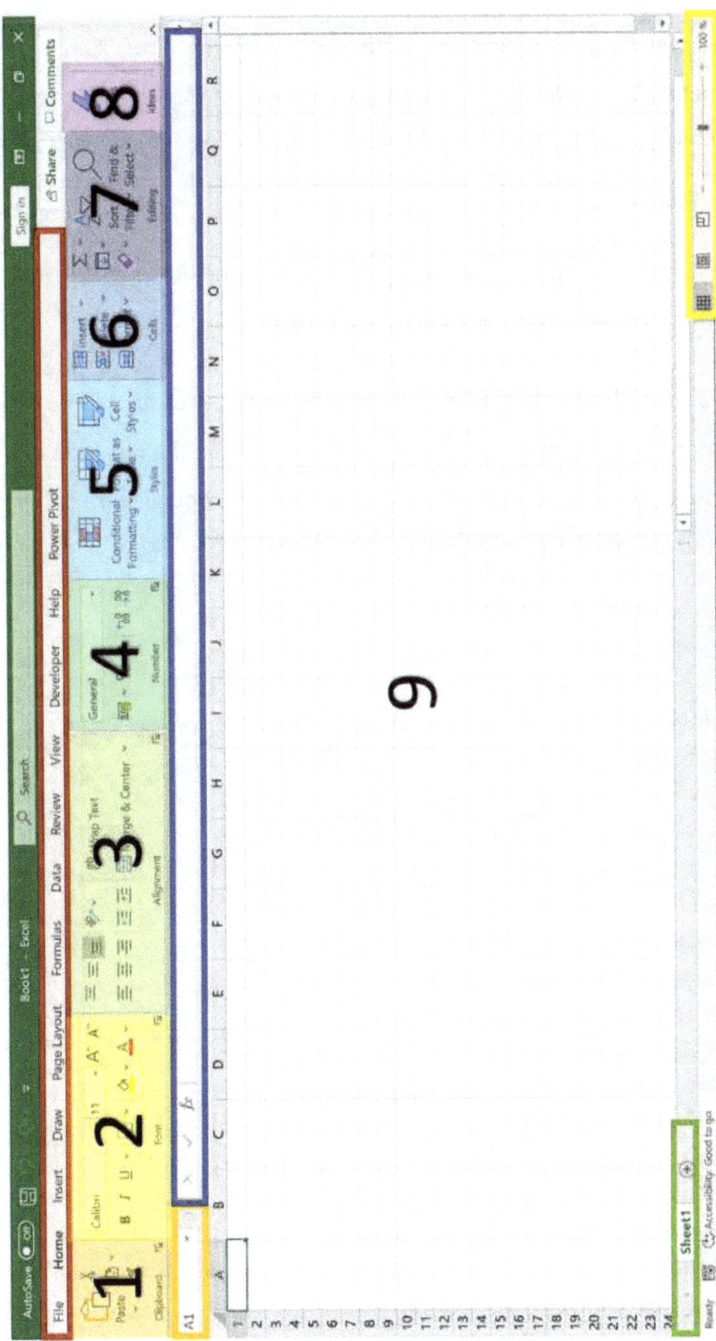

Figure 1: Excel Interface and worksheet

In **area 1** (see *Fig. 1*) you can copy, paste or cut content and use "Format painter". This function is very helpful if you want to transfer the formatting of a cell – for example: text size, **bold text**, *italic text* or even text or cell color – to one or more other cells in the same way.

In **area 2**, make settings for the font of texts, i.e., elements such as: *italic*, **bold**, underlined, font color and size, etc.

In **area 3** you will find settings for the alignment of the cell contents. You can center cell content or align it left or right. You can also change the direction of the text and "Merge cells", i.e., combine several cells into a compound and – for example – center the cell contents (see *Figure 2*).

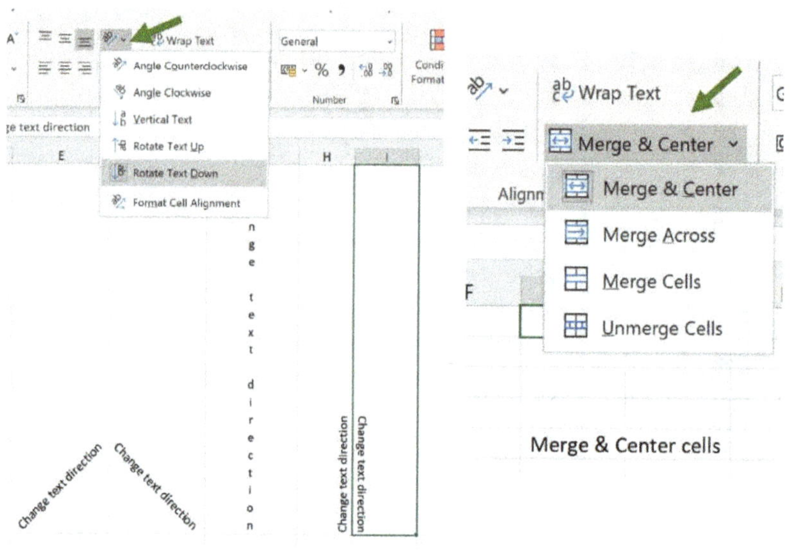

Figure 2: Change cell alignment (left) and merge cells (right)

"Number formats" can be defined in **area 4** (see *Fig. 3*). Whether currency, percent, time, fractions or exponential number. No problem for Excel. Further, formats such as special formats can be found by clicking on "More number formats..." in the lower area.

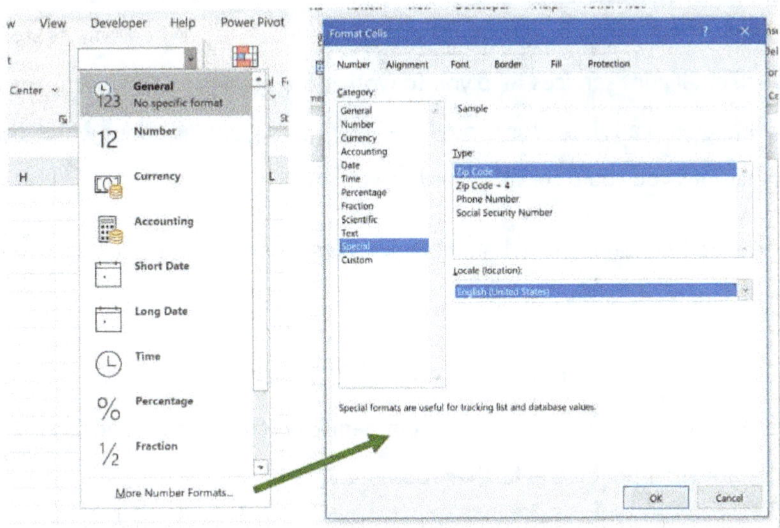

Figure 3: Determine number format (left). More number formats (right)

In **areas 5** and **6** you can easily change the formatting using templates as well as insert and modify cells/columns. We will come to the specific functions of these areas later in the book.

In **area 7** (Editing) you will find shortcuts for frequently used functions such as "Calculate Sum", "Calculate Average", "Find Max/Min", "Sort", "Filter", "Find & Replace" and others. These functions will also be explained in more detail throughout the book. A very helpful function to delete formatting is also to be found here (see *Fig. 4*).

Figure 4: "Clear"-function (formatting, contents, comments, links)

In **area 8**, Excel offers a special function called "Ideas". When this feature is enabled, intelligent services help you to work more productively. This means that when you create a table – for example – you get suggestions about which charts or evaluations you could create regarding your data.

Finally, **area 9** contains the actual table. It consists of rows and columns arranged in an alphanumeric order.

1.2 Recommended Settings

In this chapter, you will find some recommended settings and extensions. These settings are essential for the further content of the book.

Go to the settings as shown in *Fig. 5* via the tab "File" -> "Options" (ribbon). Then select the tab "Customize Ribbon" in the pop-up window and activate all functions in the right area, especially "Developer" and "Add-Ins" (also make sure that you have selected "All Tabs" in the upper-right corner).

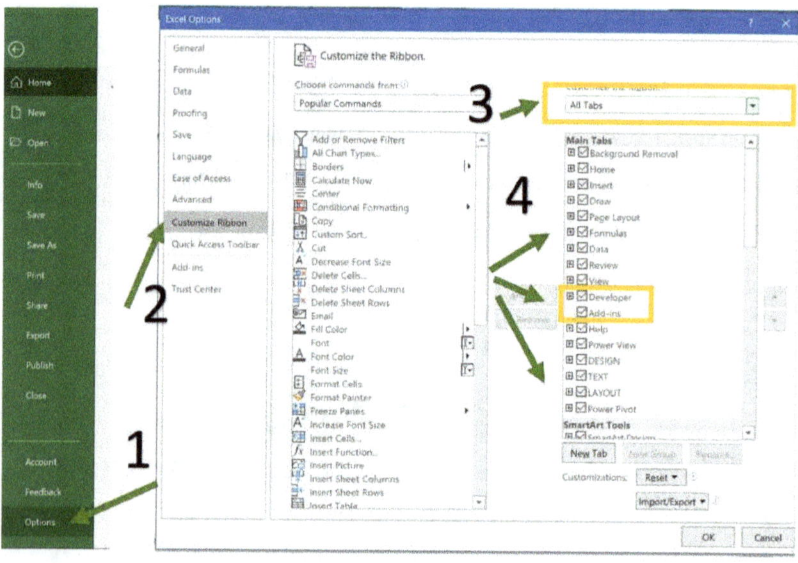

Figure 5: "Customize Ribbon" in "Excel Options"

Additionally, activate all relevant COM Add-Ins as shown in *Fig. 6.*

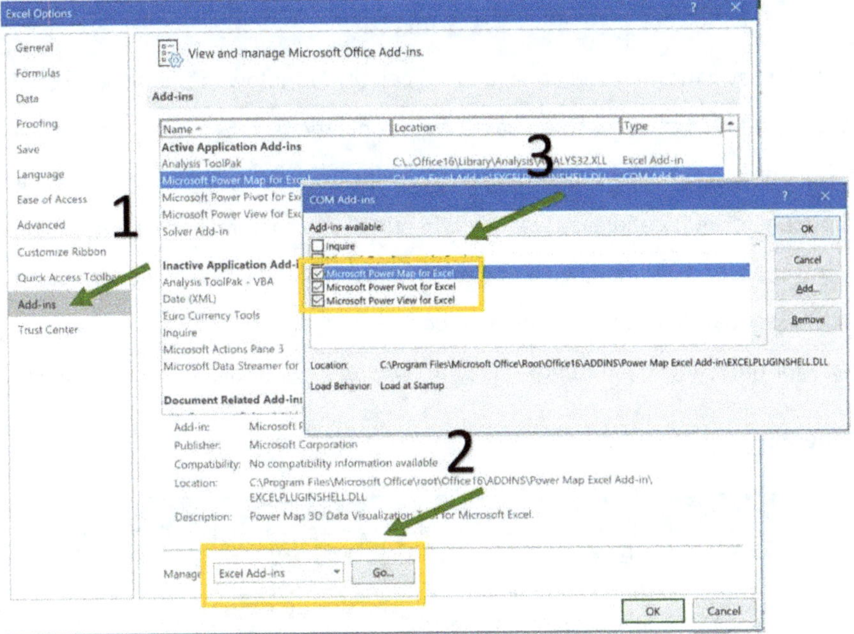

Figure 6: Activate relevant COM Add-Ins

2 Start, Basic-Tips & Shortcuts

2.1 Shortcuts

To make navigation in Excel easier and to keep the workflow as smooth as possible, it is a good idea to know some basic key combinations in Excel (it is best to even know some of them by heart). The following is a list of the most important shortcuts for quick and easy working. Try out all the combinations, some of them you will probably remember automatically. To make it even easier for you, the most essential shortcuts are marked green.

Note for the following: + stands for "and", whereby "+" stands for the actual plus.

General:

Function	Shortcut
Save document	CTRL + S
Copy	CTRL + C
Paste	CTRL + V
Select all	CTRL + A
Delete all	CTRL + R (prior: CTRL + A)
Cut (clipboard)	CTRL + X
Undo	CTRL + Z
Redo	CTRL + Y

Navigation within an Excel document:

Function	Shortcut
Choose top/bottom line	CTRL + Arrow keys up/down
Choose leftmost/rightmost column	CTRL + Arrow keys left/right
Navigation to first cell	CTRL + POS 1
Navigation to last cell	CTRL + END
Extend cell selection	SHIFT + Arrow keys
Find	CTRL + F

Formatting of sheet/cells:

Function	Shortcut
Line break in cell	ALT + ENTER
Insert columns/rows	CTRL + "+"
Delete columns/rows	CTRL + "-"
Edit selected cell	F2

Copy & Paste:

Function	Shortcut
Insert new worksheet	SHIFT + F11
Insert current date	CTRL + "."
Insert current time	CTRL + ":"
Insert/change comment	SHIFT + F2
Insert Link	CTRL + K

Formulas & Functions:

Function	Shortcut
Sum over row/column	ALT + "=" (ALT + SHIFT + 0)
Convert relative cell references into absolute ones	F4 (Select Cell selection bar at the top)
Apply format: "Currency"	CTRL + $
Apply format: "Percentage"	CTRL + %
Apply format: "Standard"	CTRL + &
Calculate active worksheet	SHIFT + F9
Calculate all worksheets	F9
Select "Quick-Analysis tool"	CTRL + Q

2.2 Quick-Analysis Tool

Using the Quick-Analysis tool, you can quickly and easily format, create charts, calculate results and perform other analyses. To access the Quick Analysis window, select a range of data and click on the small icon in the lower-right corner (see *Figure 7*) or alternatively click **CTRL + Q**. For simple data sets, this is one of the fastest ways to create professional analyses (see *Fig. 8*).

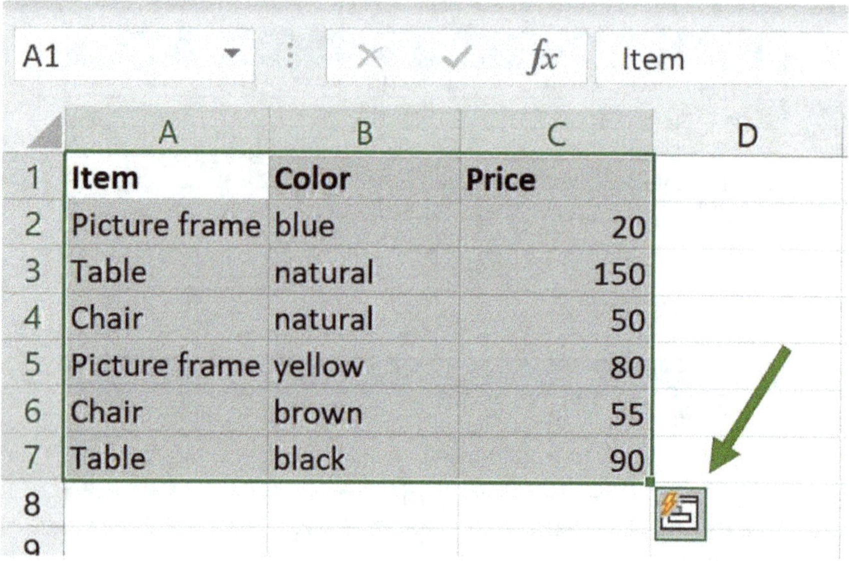

Figure 7: How to use the "Quick-Analysis" Tool

Fig. 8 shows a selection of essential functions. For example, you can insert data bars (top left) or a color scale into your data set. This enhances the visual presentation and increases the clarity of your data sets. Furthermore, you can have a totals row created (bottom left display) or a chart created (right display).

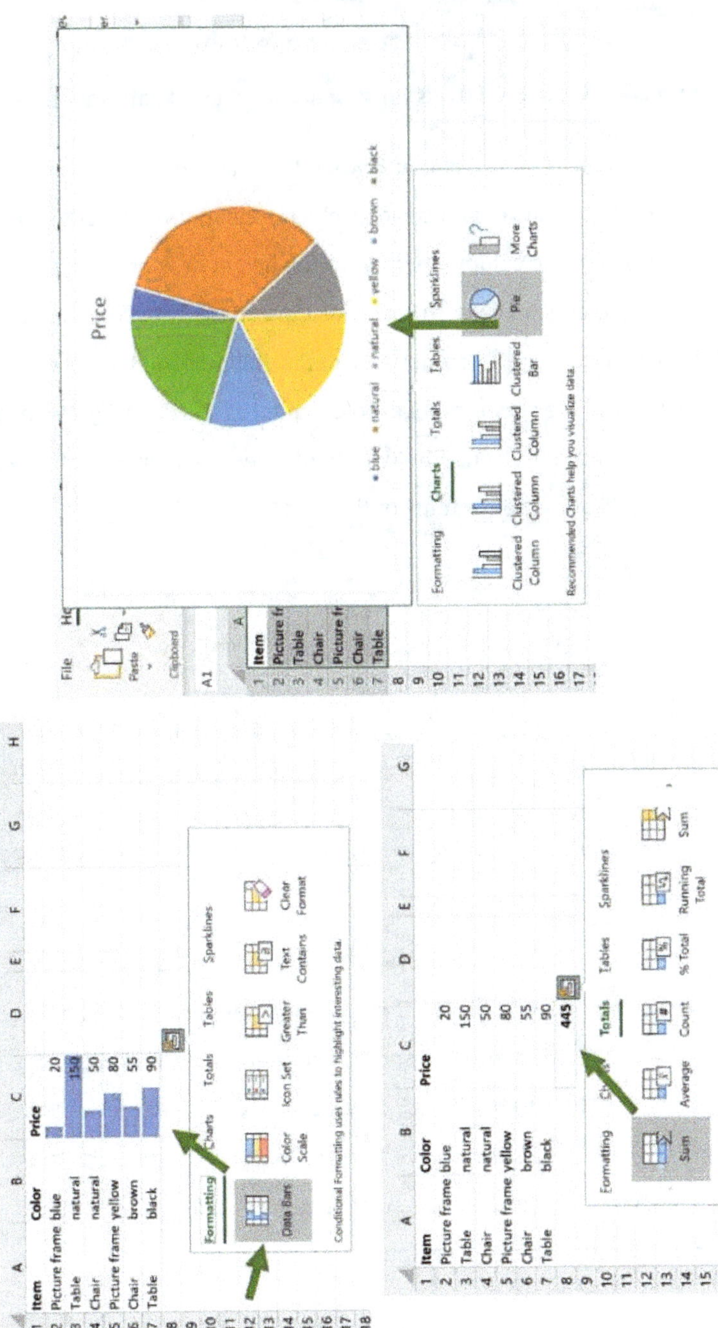

Figure 8: Some functions of the "Quick-analysis" tool

2.3 Formatting in a Nutshell

This chapter contains helpful tricks for formatting an Excel data sheet.

2.3.1 Adjust Column & Row Width automatically

In order to create a uniform and clear Excel data sheet, it is very advantageous to automatically adjust the columns & rows to the height or width of the content. To do this, move the cursor of your mouse into the space between two columns or rows as shown in *Fig. 9* in the border area of the columns (A, B, C, …) or rows (1, 2, 3, …) and wait until the cursor changes to a symbol as shown in *Fig. 9*. Double-click with the left mouse button. The width of the rows or columns will then automatically adjust to the contents of the cells.

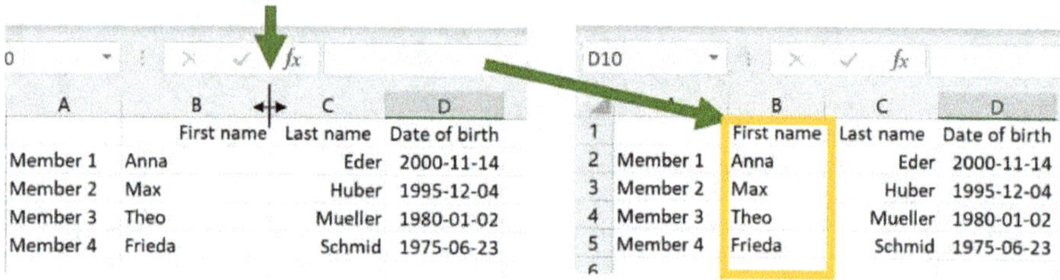

Figure 9: Waiting for cursor icon (left image), double click, column width adjusted (right image)

2.3.2 Insert Options

To swap rows and columns, i.e., to transpose the data or to create links between datasets, there are special insert options. Use them as follows: Copy the desired data (select and **CTRL + C**), then click on an empty cell (right click) and select one of the insert options as shown in *Figure 10*. In *Figure 11* you can see that the records have been inserted transposed or linked. You can easily test these links by changing the values in the original data set.

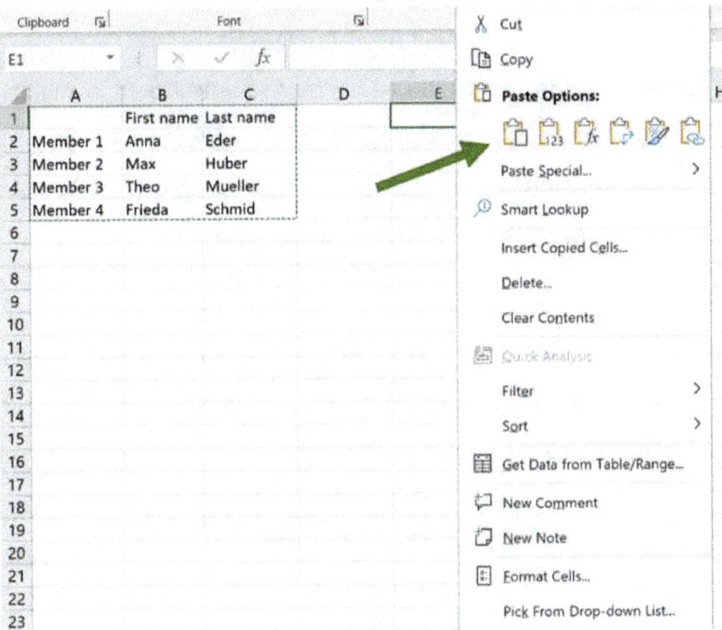

Figure 10: Insert Options

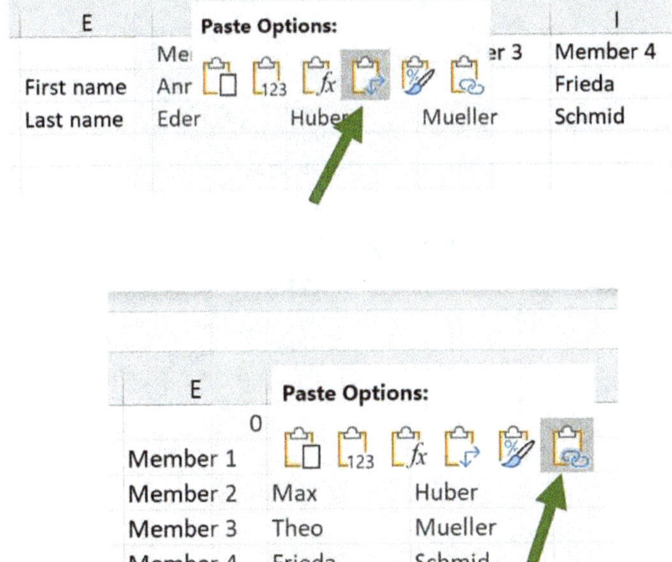

Figure 11: Transpose (top) or link (bottom) data sets

2.3.3 Autofill & Pattern Recognition

Excel's Autofill function assists you in inserting identical data in multiple rows and/or columns. All you have to do is "grab" a cell at the small dot at the bottom right with the cursor (click on the small dot) and drag it over the desired rows/columns (mouse button remains pressed; see *Fig. 12*).

On the other hand, Excel is also a master in pattern recognition, which brings many advantages for the user. For example, you can let Excel complete data series starting with just two filled cells. To do this, select two cells and proceed as described in the first paragraph (see *Figure 13*).

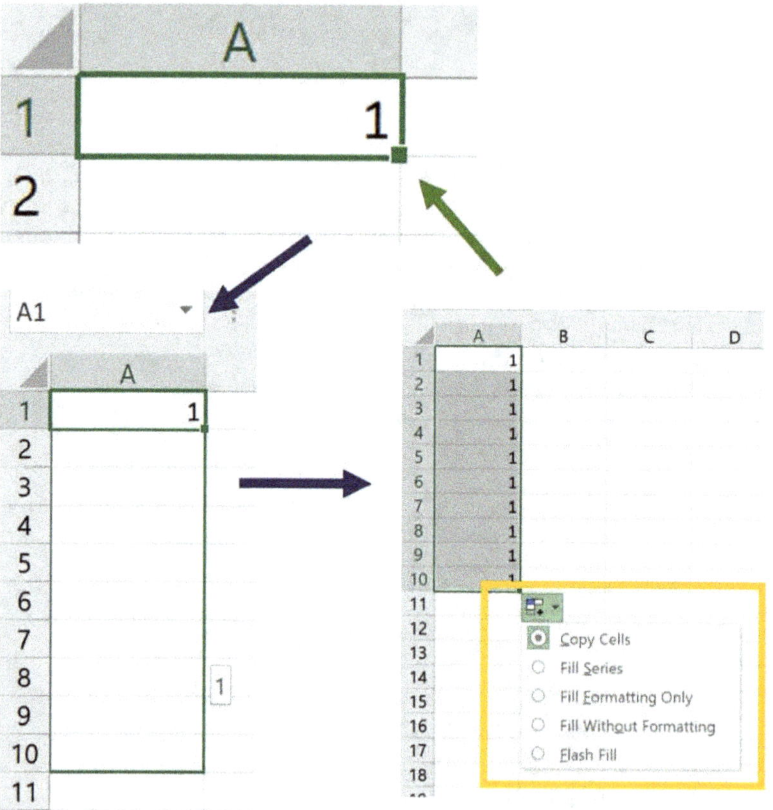

Figure 12: Auto-Fill

In the drop-down menu (*Figs. 12 & 13*; framed in orange) you can choose between further options. For example, you could fill in the "formats only" or fill in "without formats" (*Fig. 13*).

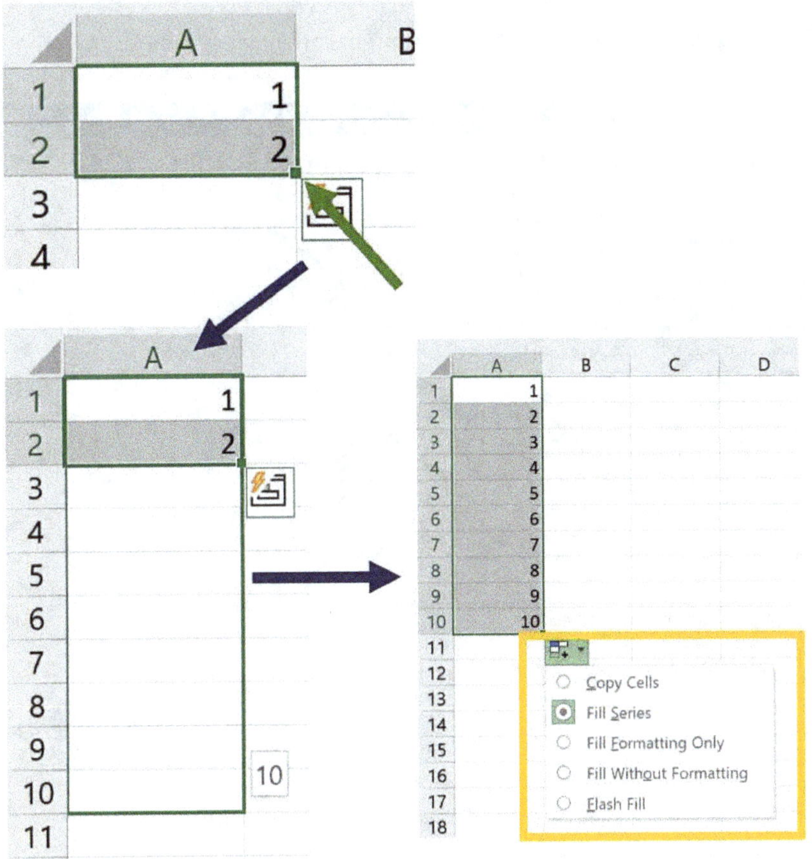

Figure 13: Pattern Recognition

2.3.4 Cell Name & Hide Cell Value

You can – as mentioned at the beginning – name each cell individually. The only thing you have to keep in mind is that you have to use the new name for each reference to this cell.

The cell value can also be hidden – e.g., from prying eyes. This works as follows: Select one or more cells and right-click. Then select "Format cells..." in the lower area. A pop-up window will open. In this pop-up window, select "Custom" in the left-hand area and enter three semicolons in the right-hand field "Type" (orange): ";;;". After confirming with "Ok" the cell contents are hidden (see *Fig. 14*).

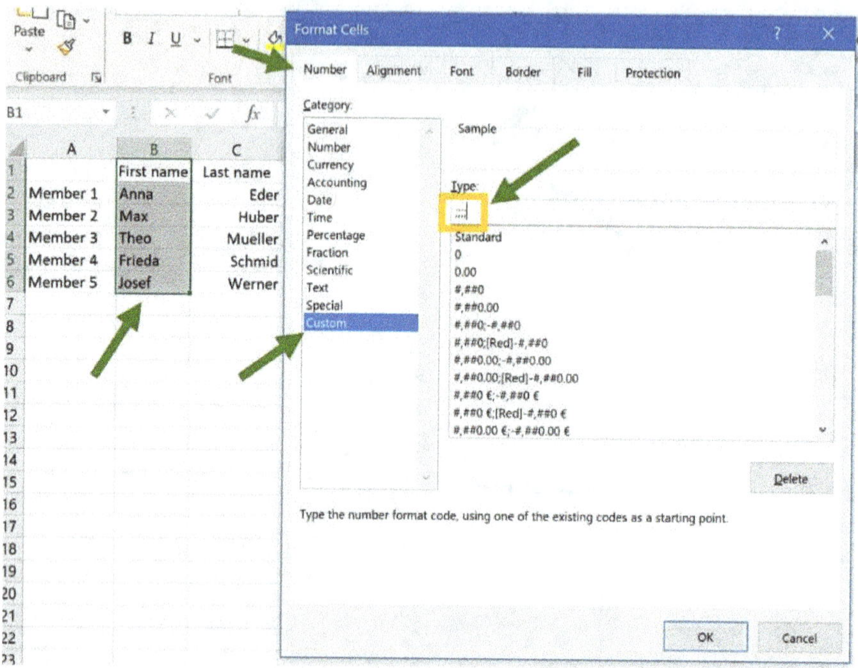

Figure 14: Hide cell contents via "Format cells"

In the upper row (function row), however, the contents appear when the cell is selected. The hiding process can be easily undone by selecting the original formatting, e.g., "Standard".

2.4 Unit Conversion

Converting units quickly is possible with the function "=CONVERT". Use this function as shown in *Fig. 15*. A pre-selection of conversion terms is displayed when filling in the function arguments.

An extended conversion of data, as it is necessary for example for currency conversion (exchange rate changes), will be explained in **Chapter 3**.

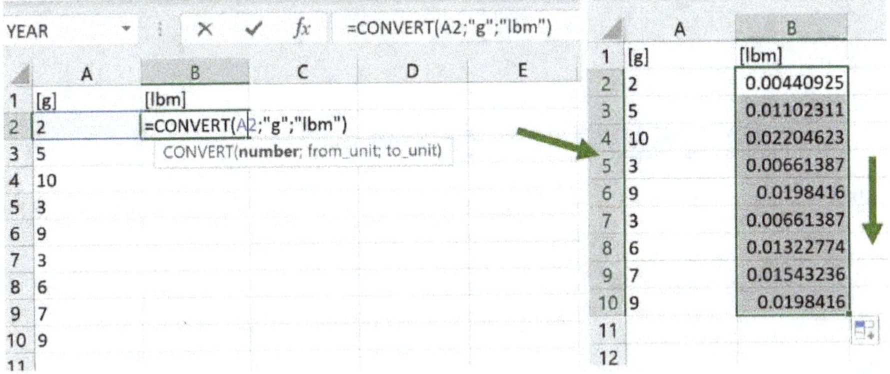

Figure 15: Conversion of units with "=CONVERT"

You can then drag the function over other areas (see "Autofill" in **Chapter 2.3.3**) and they will be converted as well. An introduction to formulas and how to use important formulas correctly can be found in **Chapter 6**.

2.5 Find and Replace

The option "Find & Replace" is needed if you want to replace identical terms in a relatively large Excel worksheet. Here you can avoid the effort of manually searching and replacing. Excel can do this for you automatically. To do so, select "Find & Select" from the "Home" section in the upper right-hand corner under the small magnifying glass (see *Fig. 16*). Select the tab "Replace" in the pop-up window (alternatively, you can also use "Find" for searching purposes only). Then expand the window via "Options" and finally type the search term in the field "Find what" and the replacement term in the field below (framed in orange; step 2). If it is important to replace only the actual search term or if the search is case-sensitive, check the respective boxes (green frame). *Attention: If you do <u>not</u> activate "Match entire cell contents", for words like "dog" replacing "do" with "don`t", will cause "don`tg". This will obviously lead to misresults.*

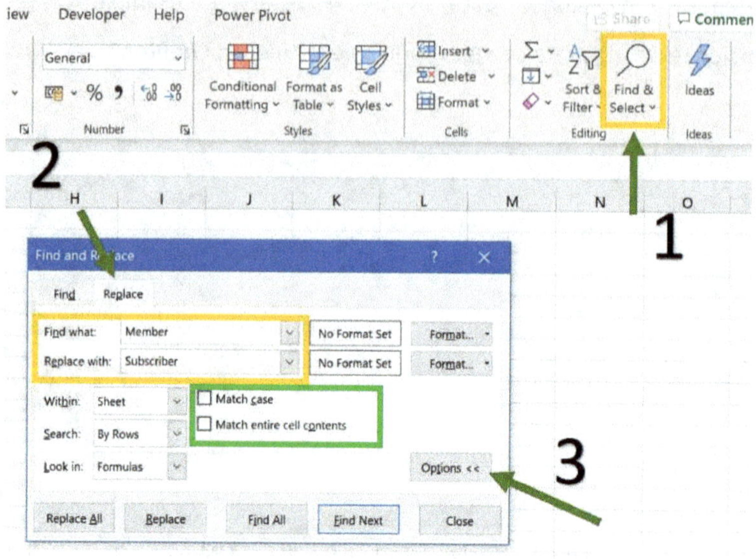

Figure 16: "Find & Replace"

2.6 Sort

With the feature "Sort" you can easily sort complete data sets by criteria such as alphabetical order, date, etc. Please refer to *Figure 17*. Select a range and choose "Sort..." or "Custom Sort...".

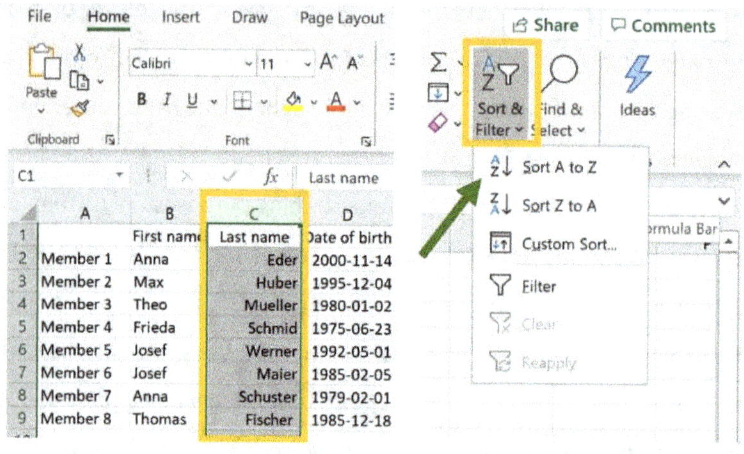

Figure 17: Sort data in alphabetical order

2.7 Conditional Formatting

You can format data according to conditions. This means that you can automatically assign a specific format (font color, cell color, etc.) to cells that meet the conditions you defined beforehand. For example, as shown in *Figure 18*, you can highlight all values in a column that are "Greater than..." or "Less than..." a certain value.

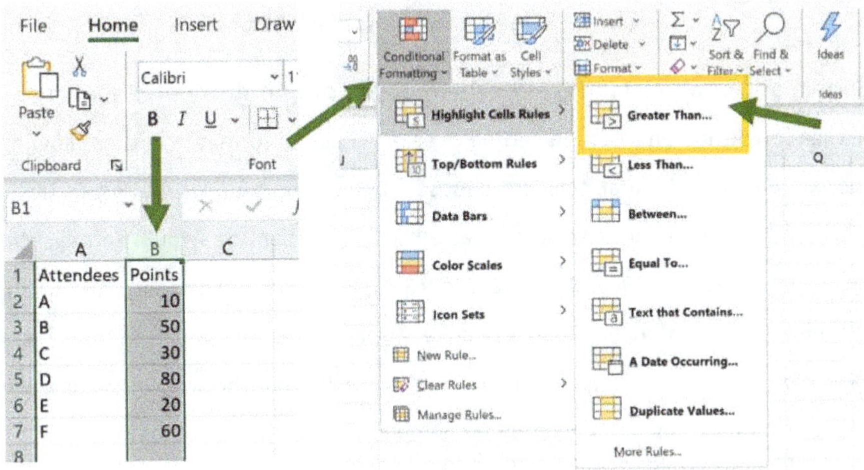

Figure 18: Conditional Formatting using "Greater than..."

If you select "Greater than..." or one of the other conditions, a pop-up window as shown in *Fig. 19* will open, where you can enter the value (framed in orange) that represents your condition. In this example, all values greater than 45 should be marked red.

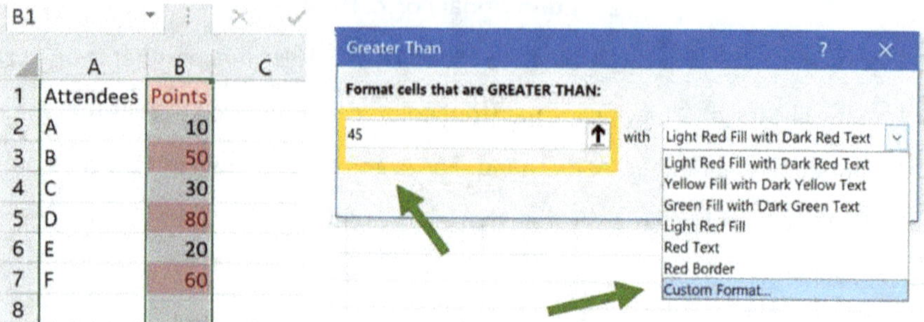

Figure 19: "Greater than..." and format settings

In the drop-down menu (*Fig. 19* right-side) you can set the desired formatting. Either you decide on a default setting or select "Custom format..." in the following pop-up window "Format cells" to choose from a variety of formatting settings. Furthermore, data can also be formatted with data bars or symbol sets can be inserted, as shown in *Fig. 20*. It is best to try out all formatting options. In addition, depending on the data set, the respective formatting options will fit better or less well. You can also create and manage your own rules, but this will be explained in a later chapter using a more complex example.

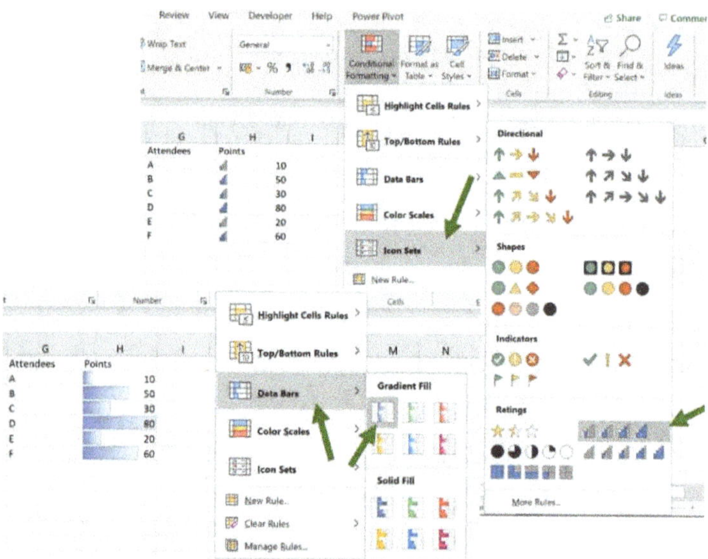

Figure 20: Options for conditional formatting (data bars or symbol sets)

3 Insert

3.1 Tables

3.1.1 Simple Tables

In this chapter, we will first discuss simple tables. To insert a simple table, first select the data set and then either create the table using the Quick Analysis Tool or by using the shortcut CTRL+T or by clicking the "Table" button in the ribbon (section "Insert"; see *Fig. 21*).

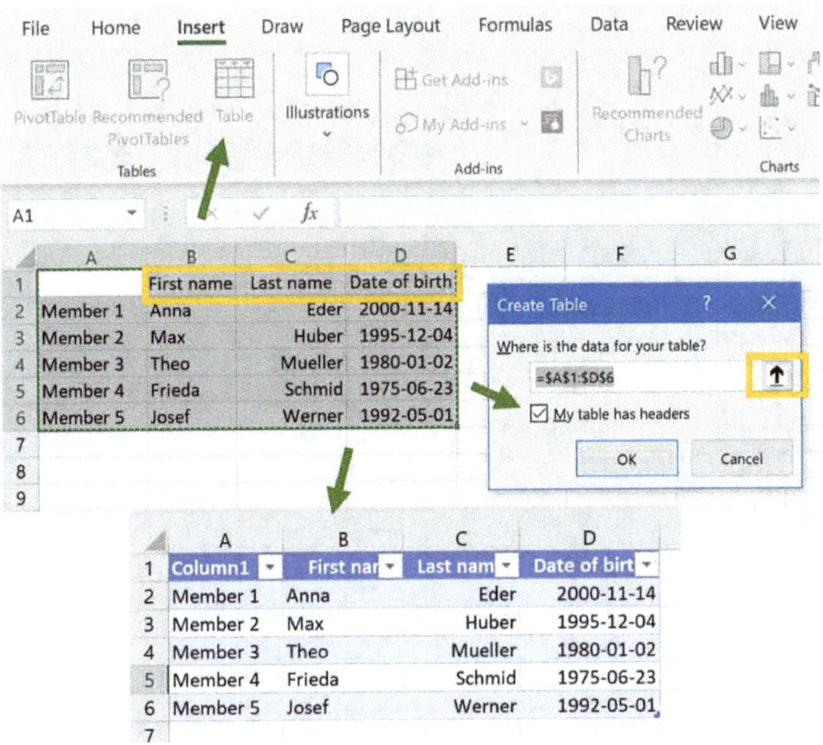

Figure 21: Creating a table via the ribbon section "Insert"

You can also change the selection of the data set using the small black arrow pointing upwards (framed in orange). If you check the small box "...table has headers", the program recognizes the first line as a header and automatically applies the option "filter". In the respective drop-down menu, you can select which data should be displayed. If you want to evaluate or display a large amount of data, use a pivot table. This special table type can be found to the left of the item "Table" (ribbon: "Insert").

3.1.2 PivotTables

As shown in Fig. 22, select a desired data range and create a pivot table by clicking the corresponding button "PivotTable". In the pop-up window that opens, change the data selection if necessary and define the target area of the table. In this case, we select "New worksheet".

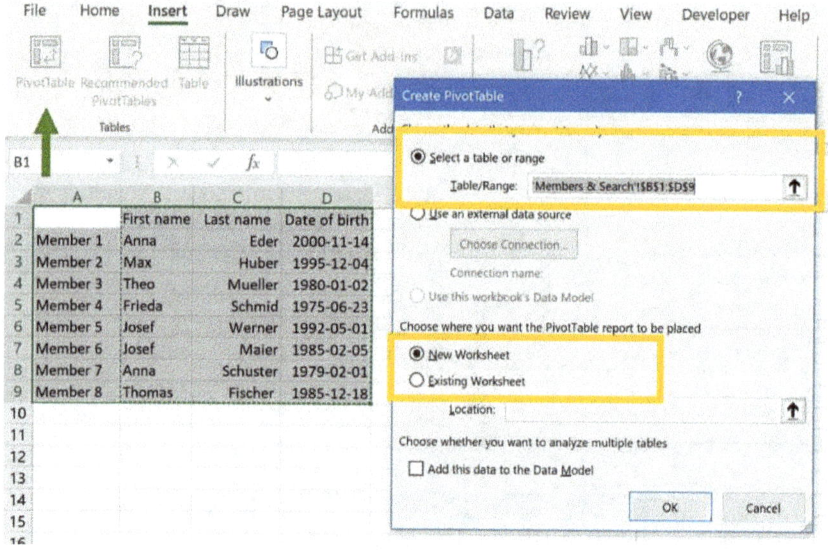

Figure 22: Creating a PivotTable

As defined, the pivot table opens in a new worksheet. As shown in Fig. 23, in the right-hand area you must then select which data you want to display. You can sort or summarize this data as you wish. In the selection area (right margin) you will find the option of selecting data (framed in orange) and below it the areas "Filters", "Columns", "Rows" and "Values" (see Fig. 23). These can be used to control the clear arrangement and reduction of the data. Let us understand this better by using an example.

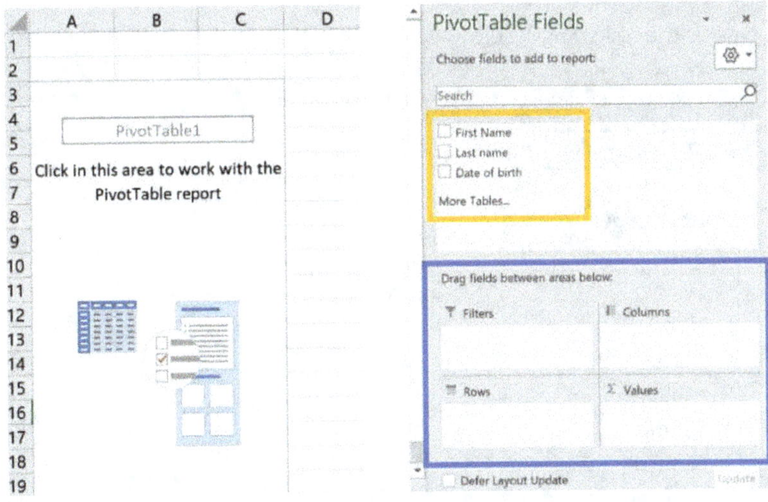

Figure 23: Selection options when creating a PivotTable

For example, we want to present our data in such a way that we can display all members of our organization having a certain first name. So, we filter for a particular first name and as a result, we can display all matching last names. We can proceed as follows: If you select all "First names" as in *Fig. 24* (step 1; top), they will appear in the section "Rows" (*Fig. 23*; step 1, bottom), since these are line entries of the original data set. Now we can click on "First names" and select "Move to report filter" to move them to the area "Filters" (*Fig. 24*; step 2). Finally, check the box of "Last names", which will then also appear in "Rows" (*Fig. 24*; step 3).

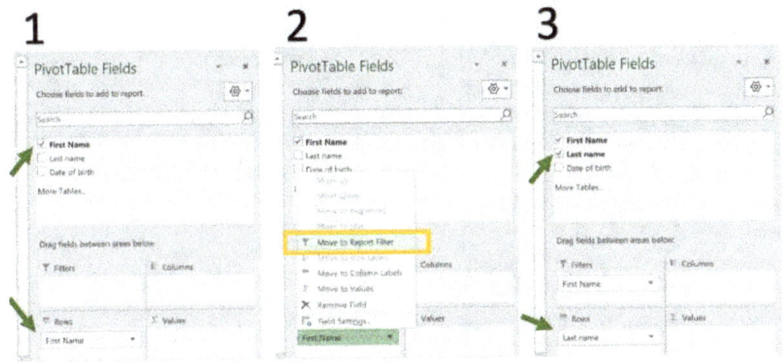

Figure 24: PivotTable fields step by step (left to right)

This gives us the following result:

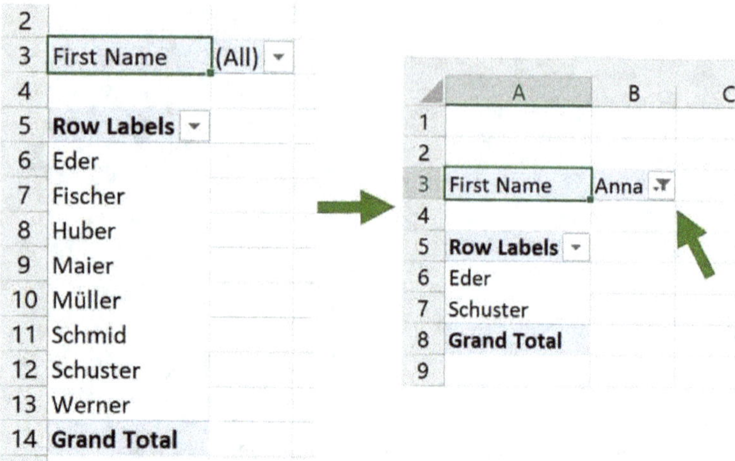

Figure 25: Complete pivot table with filtering function

As shown in *Fig. 25*, a name can now be selected in the "First name" field, and all surnames assigned to this first name will then be displayed. Goal achieved! We can also include an automatic counting function or summation In this example. Try doing this with help of what is shown in *Fig. 26*. **Hint:** To do this, right-click on Last Name in the selection field and select "Move to values". This will show us the number and its total (see *Fig. 26*).

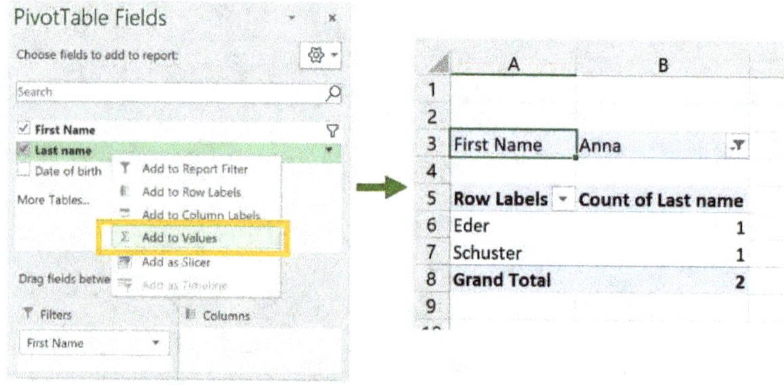

Figure 26: "Move to values" to display number and total

3.2 Illustrations and Add-Ins

In the menu item "Illustrations" you can insert or create all kinds of images, symbols, shapes or SmartArts. If you want your Excel workbook to look more vivid, this is the proper section for you. Either insert your own images or choose from Excel templates. Particularly worth mentioning are the shapes (*Fig. 27*),

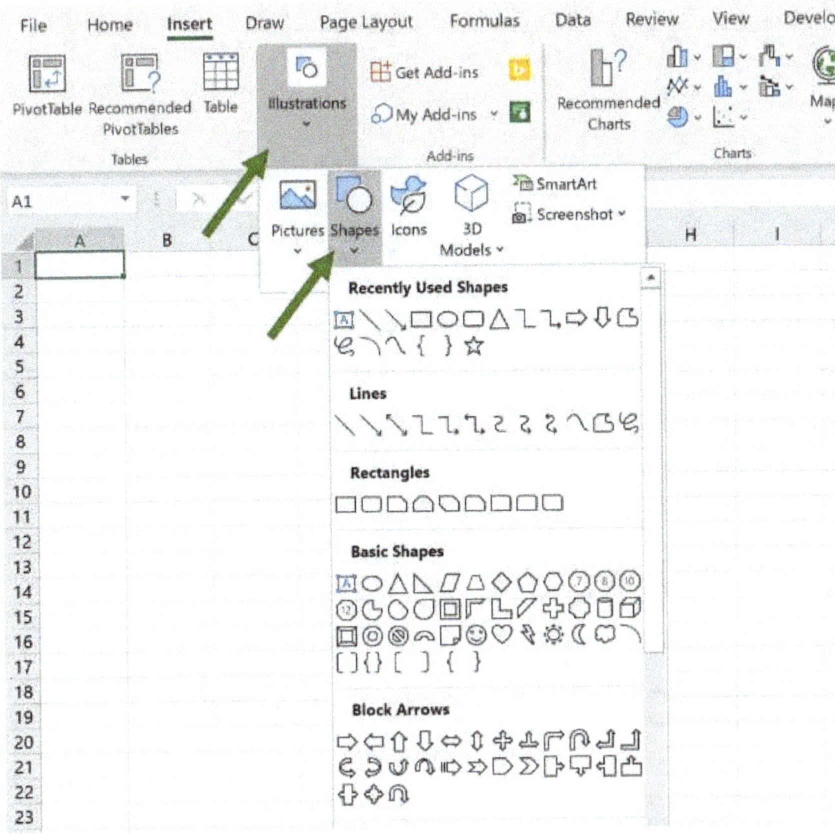

Figure 27: Overview of "Shapes"

special symbols and SmartArts (see *Fig. 28*).

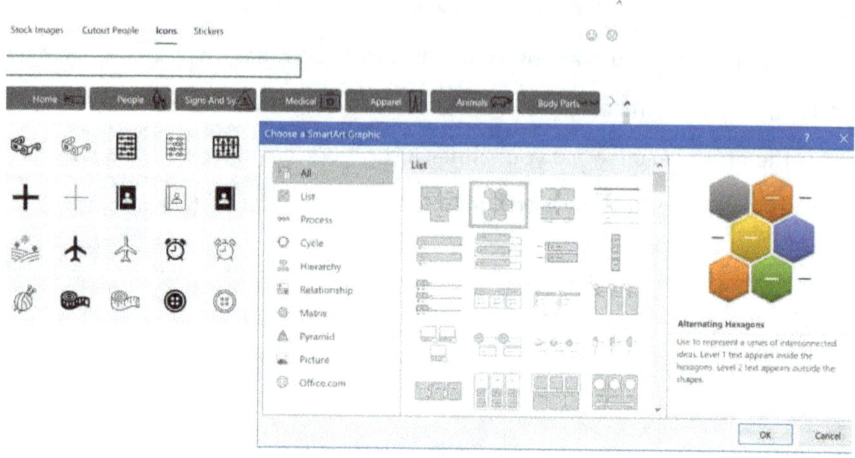

Figure 28: Insert "Symbols" or select "SmartArts"

In the section "Add-Ins" there is another feature that is particularly worth mentioning. The Add-In "People Graph" (see *Fig. 29*). If you do not have this Add-in, you may need to install it from the Office Store. You may also need to click "Trust this Add-In" the first time you start it to use it.

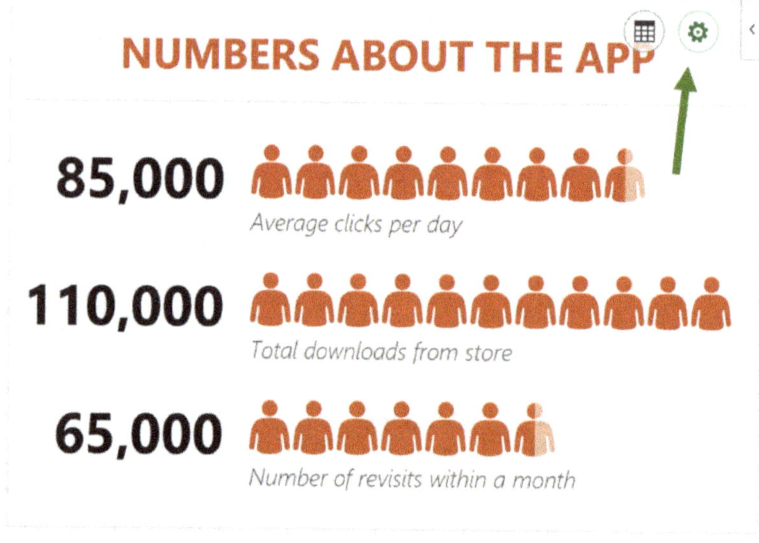

Figure 29: Prime example of the "People Graph"

"People Graph" is always useful if you want to display a lot of information about the number of processes, as in *Fig. 29* with information about the use of an app. Such an illustration is really impressive, it looks very professional. If you move the mouse to the right edge, two small windows appear (see *Fig. 29*). You can use the left window to select the data (*Fig. 30*) and the right window to adjust the add-in settings to your needs (*Fig. 31*). Try it right away!

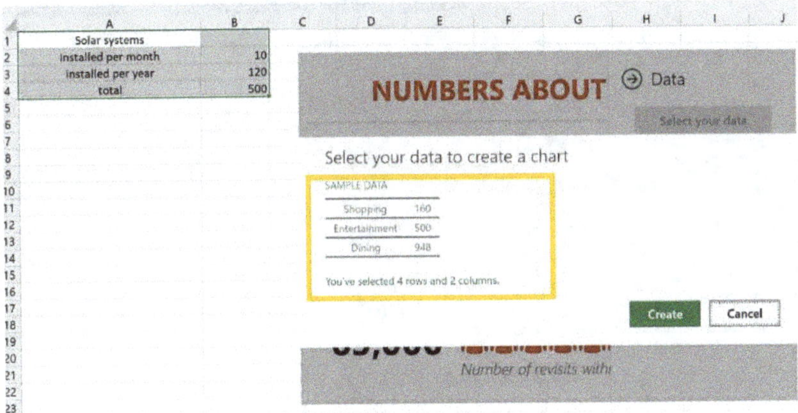

Figure 30: Selecting data for "People Graph"

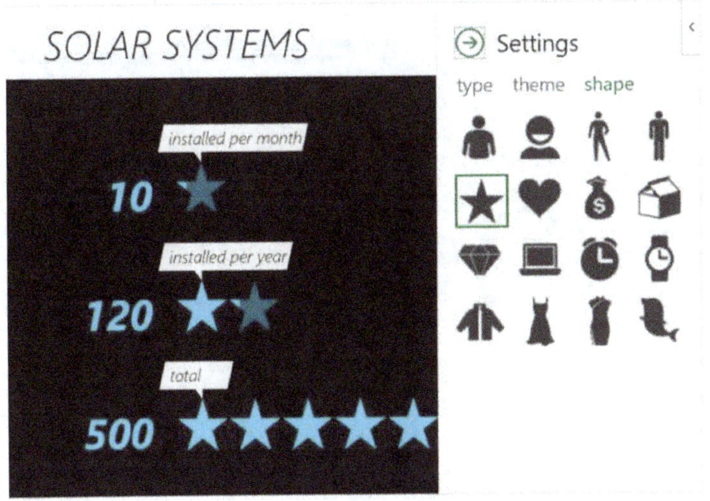

Figure 31: Settings for "Type", "Theme" & "Shape"

3.3 Charts

Excel is perfect for creating charts. You can create a variety of different types. To convert a data set into a proper chart, it is advisable to use the feature "Recommended charts" at first. Excel will then suggest suitable charts (see *Figure 32*).

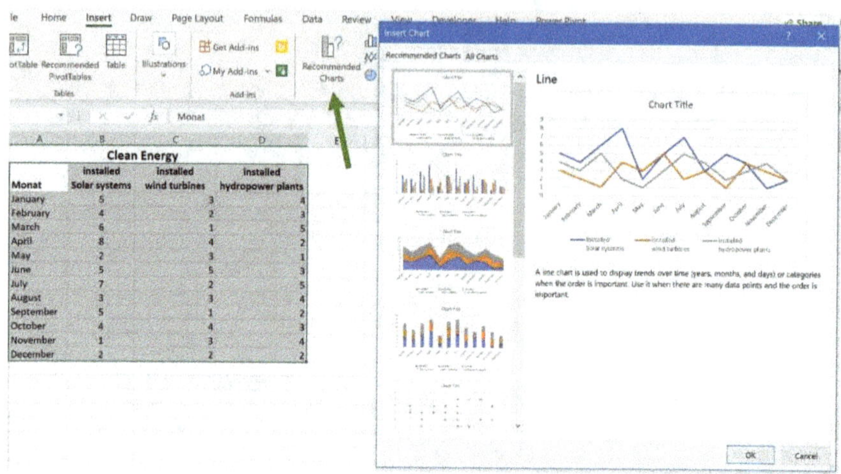

Figure 32: Using the feature "Recommended Charts"

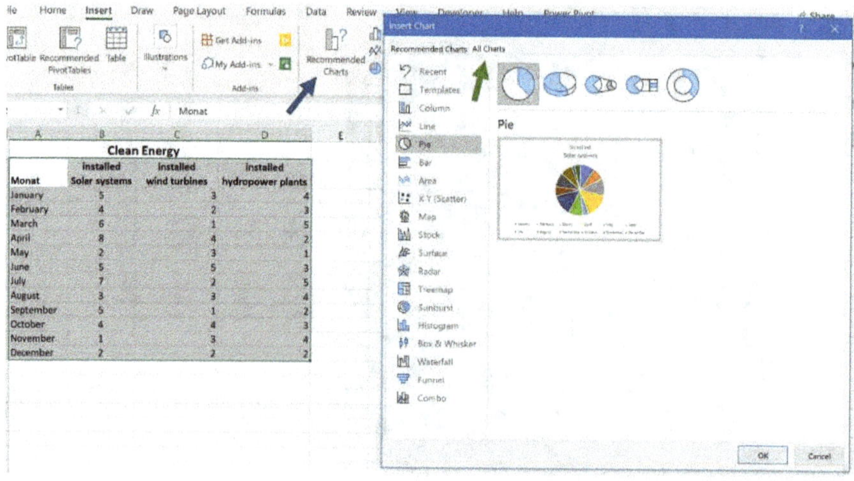

Figure 33: Choose the type of the chart

If you switch to the tab "All charts", you can display a preview of all charts available (see *Fig. 33*, green arrow). This can be very helpful for manual selection. Alternatively, you can also create certain types of charts using the small selection icons (blue arrow).

In *Fig. 34* you can see a pie chart. When you select the chart area (by double-clicking on it), several setting options appear in the upper area. First, you can add another element to the chart (framed in green). This can be a title, a legend, a label, or in case of a different chart type a trend line. In this area, you can also adjust the layout quickly. In the orange-framed area you have the option of making further adjustments that affect the appearance of the chart, and in the blue-framed area you can make changes to the data selection. Changing or moving the chart type (to the right of the blue frame) should be intuitive.

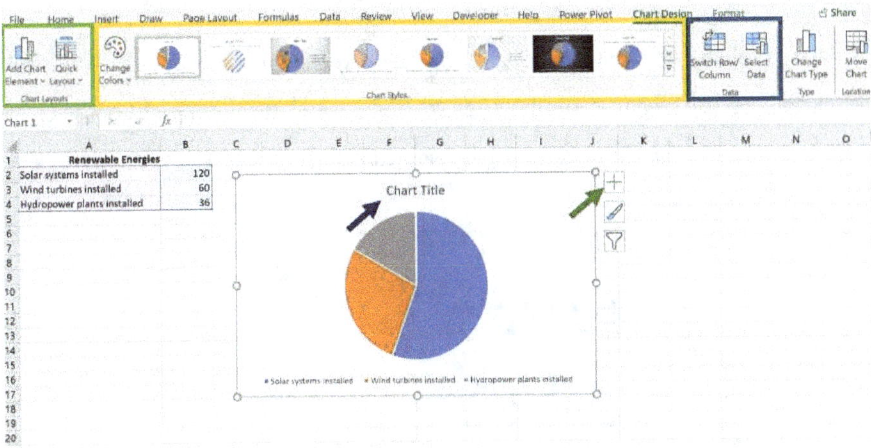

Figure 34: Setting options of a chart

Some of these settings can also be made in the chart area (green arrow). You can also edit the elements (for example, the title; blue arrow) by double-clicking on them. A window with formatting options (in the right-hand area; not shown) then opens.

Another classic chart is a line chart. As shown in *Fig. 35*, all types of trends (e.g., temporal trends) can be displayed.

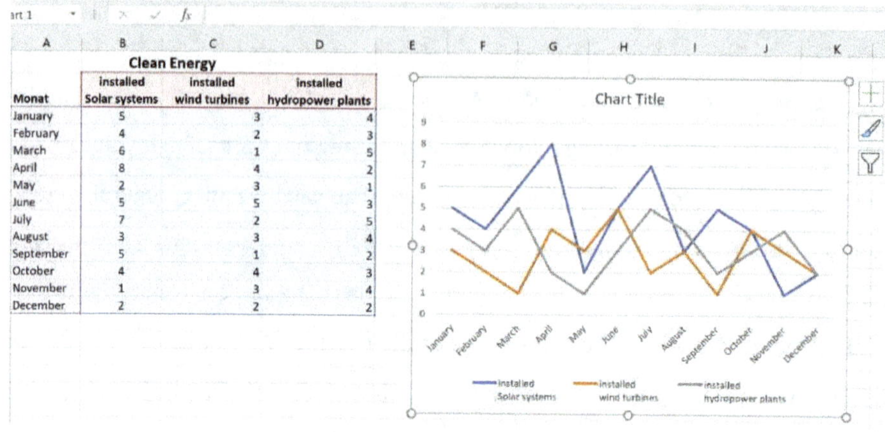

Figure 35: Line chart as a trend overview

Create a table as shown in *Fig. 35* and try it by yourself. The procedure is identical. By clicking on the small "+" symbol (*Fig. 36*, blue arrow) at the top right of the chart area, you can – as already mentioned – also add chart elements.

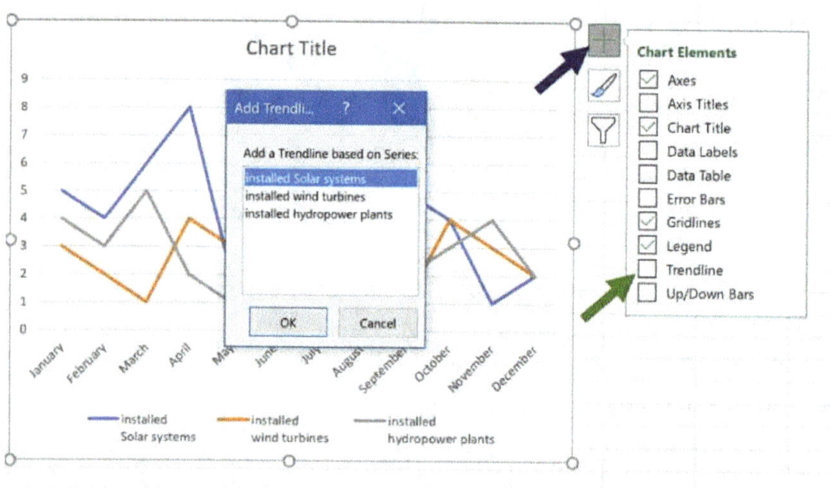

Figure 36: Add chart elements: Trend line

As for a scatter or line chart, it is useful to insert a trend line. Do this by clicking on "Trendline" (green arrow, *Fig. 36*) and selecting the desired data series (pop-up window). The result should appear as shown in *Fig. 37*. If you need another type of trend line (e.g., exponential, moving average, logarithmic or a polynomial approximation), you can change the trend line by clicking on the small black triangle (*Fig. 36*) in the right area next to the "Trend Line" check box. Also try "Further options" to see all possibilities.

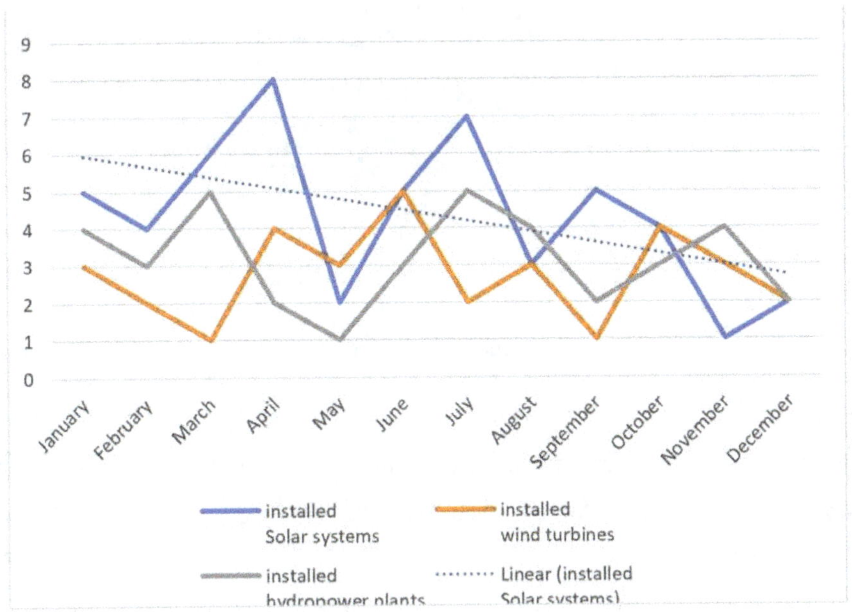

Figure 37: Created trend line (blue dotted)

If you are interested in the representation of accumulations, a radar chart is recommended. As shown in *Fig. 38*, you can see at a glance in which area the accumulations are located. In our example, this means in which month most of the plants were installed. It is created by following the same procedure as for the other chart types.

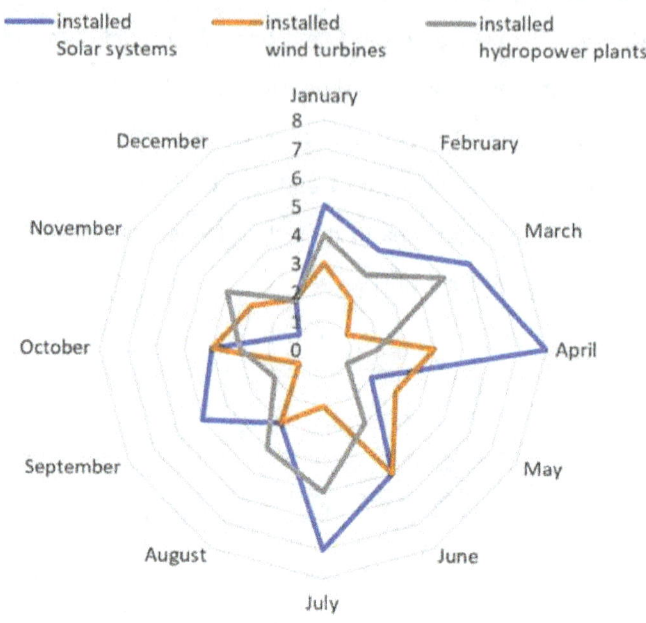

Figure 38: Radar chart

It turns out that in the months: April, July & March most of the systems were installed. Besides classical charts, you can visualize data related to countries of the world with the function "Maps". "Maps" can also be found in the section "Charts" (see *Fig. 39*).

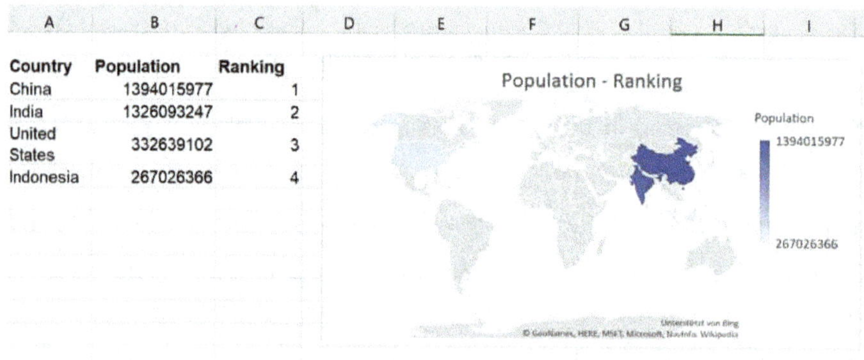

Country	Population	Ranking
China	1394015977	1
India	1326093247	2
United States	332639102	3
Indonesia	267026366	4

Figure 39: Visualization of country-specific data using "maps"

3.4 Sparklines

"Sparklines" offer the possibility to create a miniature chart in a single cell to provide a first visual impression. Create a table as shown in *Fig. 40* and generate the sparklines by selecting the data (framed in orange) and then clicking on "Line" or "Column". You have to specify the desired position (blue arrows) of the sparklines in the pop-up window. Do this by selecting a cell with your mouse.

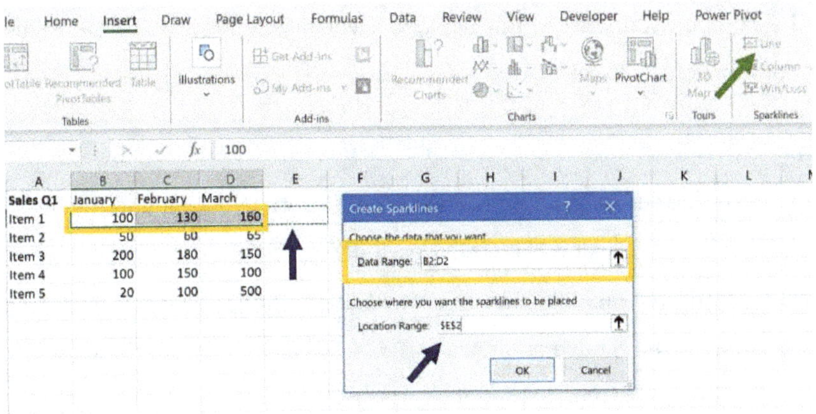

Figure 40: Creating Sparklines

As a result, you will receive the following representations:

Figure 41: Data and sparklines

For the sparklines "Win/Loss" you need values with positive and negative signs. Try it yourself! By selecting the sparklines and "Draft" in the menu bar (at the top) you can do some specific formatting. Of course, the more data you have, the more meaningful the sparklines will be. On the other hand, if there is too much data, such a small cell will become too confusing, and it is better to create a regular chart.

If you are further interested in creating charts and chart elements, you should also read a book on statistics. In this book, we would now like to turn our focus to further functions of Excel.

3.5 Slicer

If you move further to the right (ribbon area: "Insert") you will find the function "Slicer" within the section "Filters". This function is very useful if you want to display data from a table filtered by content. Let us understand this by means of an example. Create a table as shown in *Fig. 42* (select data and create the table, e.g., using the Quick Analysis Tool).

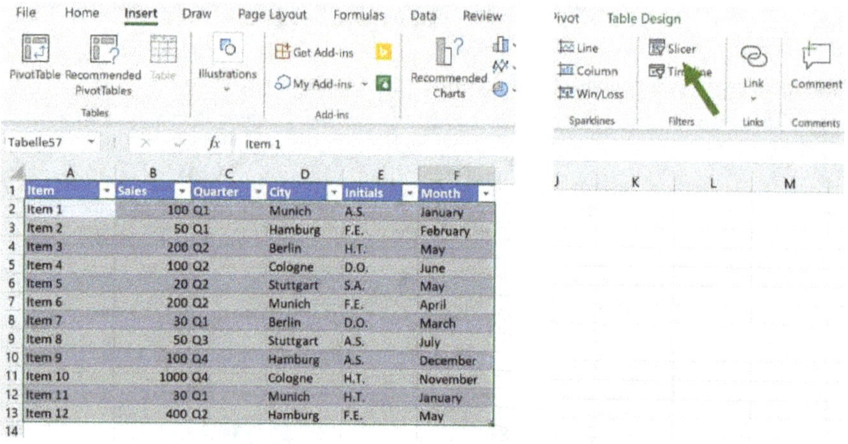

Figure 42: Creating a table and selecting "Slicer"

A selection window opens in the ribbon (top). Select the function "Insert Slicers" (alternative: "Insert" → "Filter" → "Slicer"). A pop-up window opens, in which you can select the relevant filters. For example, we would like to be able to filter by quarter, location, and seller. Therefore, select these three (*Fig. 43*; green arrow).

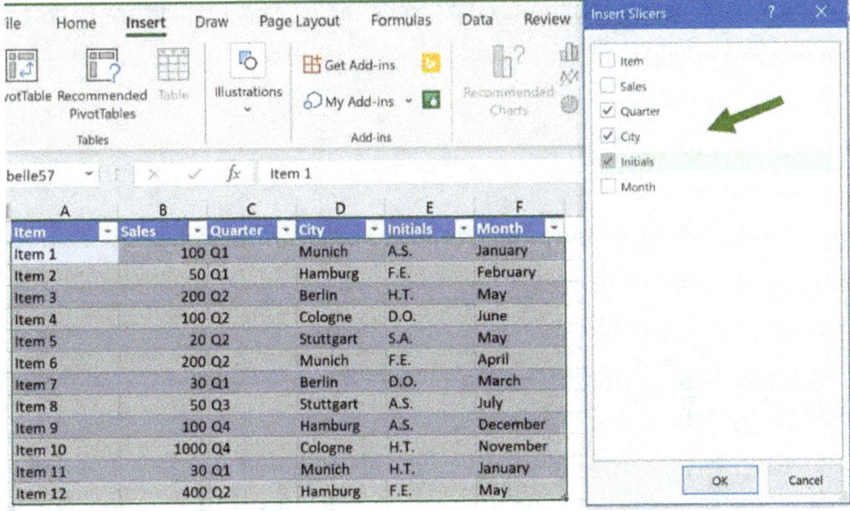

Figure 43: Selection of filters within "Insert Slicers"

Three boxes with filtering symbols and buttons (*Fig. 44*) open. By clicking on the buttons, we can now display all sold items, e.g., in "Munich".

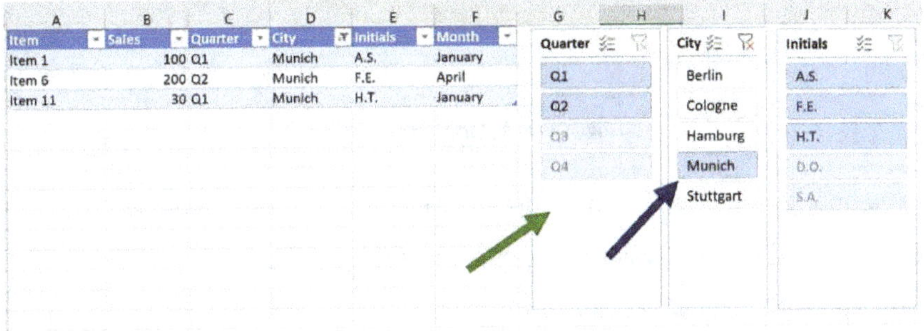

Figure 44: Filtering data using "Slicers"

By activating "Multi-select" (green arrow) in the upper part of the boxes, you can select more than one filter. You can also delete the filter in this area (blue arrow).

Using the function "Links" a little further to the right (ribbon area: "Insert") you can insert a link to another file or a visited website. The other menu items: "Comments", "Text" & "Symbols" ought to be self-explanatory and are easiest to understand by using them.

4 Draw

There is not much to mention for this ribbon segment. As shown in *Fig. 45.1*, you can use it to manually create drawings, symbols or similar visualizations in Excel.

Figure 45.1: Drawing in Excel

Furthermore, you can also remove drawings ("Eraser") or select areas with the help of a "Lasso". Besides a variety of pens, the section: "Convert" (green arrow) is particularly interesting. As the descriptions already reveal, you can let Excel transform your artistic realizations into forms and equations. An example can be found in *Figure 45.2*.

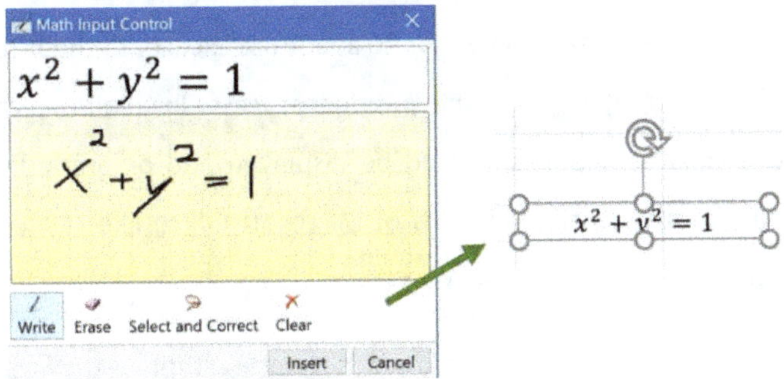

Figure 45.2: Draw a formula and let Excel do the rest

Especially for very long and complex equations, this is a fast and convenient way to insert equations or mathematical expressions. With an actual pen and a tablet, drawing will work just fine.

5 Page Layout

In the ribbon area "Page Layout" Excel will fulfill your layout desires. In the left area you can change e.g., the design, the general color composition and the fonts (see *Fig. 46*, framed in orange). The blue framed area "Page setup" you'll need if you want to modify the format, the margins, the alignment (portrait/landscape) or the print area. There you can also select a background image or a print title for your Excel worksheet.

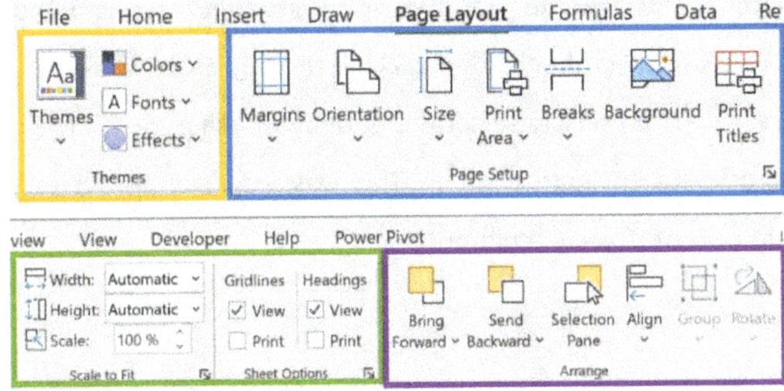

Figure 46: "Page Layout" sections

The green framed area offers the option to adapt the Excel data sheet to a defined form. This is important e.g., for the printing process. In addition, you can set whether grid lines or headings should be displayed and/or printed. The violet framed area offers standard functions of Microsoft Office like Layer settings or "Align", "Group" and "Rotate" objects.

As you see, there is not much to explain in this chapter either, as the layout settings are largely self-explanatory or well-known. Therefore, we already come to the next ribbon item: "Formulas". In this chapter, there are a lot of new things to learn.

6 Formulas

Excel is also a calculation program, so this chapter is of great importance. Many (complex) calculations can be performed easily and fast using Excel. Let's get started with some basics before we'll discuss some examples later on. In general, formulas are entered in the orange framed row in *Fig. 47* with a preceding "=". Select the cell in which the result of the formula should be displayed. With the small symbols (green arrow) to the left of the input line you can cancel an operation (also **ESC** key) or confirm it (also **ENTER** key) as well as access the function arguments via the f_x symbol. The pop-up window helps you to select the components of the respective functions or to choose the correct function. In *Fig. 47*, for example, the average grade of some students is calculated using the function "= AVERAGE(Number1,Number2)". If there is more than one data – as in this example – you can simply select the data by marking it with the mouse. The same result offers a ":" instead of ";". This way, you can always select a range between two cells of a row or column.

YEAR	▼	× ✓ $f\!x$	=AVERAGE(B2:D2)	
	A	B	C	D	E
1	Student	Math points	Language points	Art points	Average
2	Thomas	10	30	20	B2:D2)
3	Klaus	20	20	30	23.3
4	Frieda	10	10	20	13.3
5	Thorsten	30	50	40	40.0
6	Sven	20	30	50	33.3
7	Claudia	50	20	10	26.7
8	Lisa	20	10	20	16.7

Figure 47: Input of a function (example: "=AVERAGE")

6.1 Relative and Absolute Cell References

If you now let Excel complete the fields below the cell "E2" (drag down; already done in Fig. 47) you can see that the cell references automatically change row by row. I.e. "B2:D2" becomes "B3:D3" one row below, and so on. Excel recognizes a pattern and the cell references are adjusted automatically, since this is a relative cell reference.

However, if you got a constant that you need for several multiplications or other arithmetic operations, you can use an absolute cell reference. For an absolute cell reference, you must surround the letter of the cell name with "$". For example, you would write "$G$1" for cell "G1" (row and column fixed) as shown in Figure 48. If you would not do this and let Excel complete the table, Excel would use the wrong pattern (orange framed & green arrows in *Figure 48*). This way you would not get any values calculated or errors displayed as Excel attempts to calculate "C3=B3*G2", "C4=B4*G3", etc. However, the value for the discount is fixed in "F1", the other cells are empty. Hence, the absolute cell reference. Try it once without and once with "$" sign, then you will see the difference more clearly.

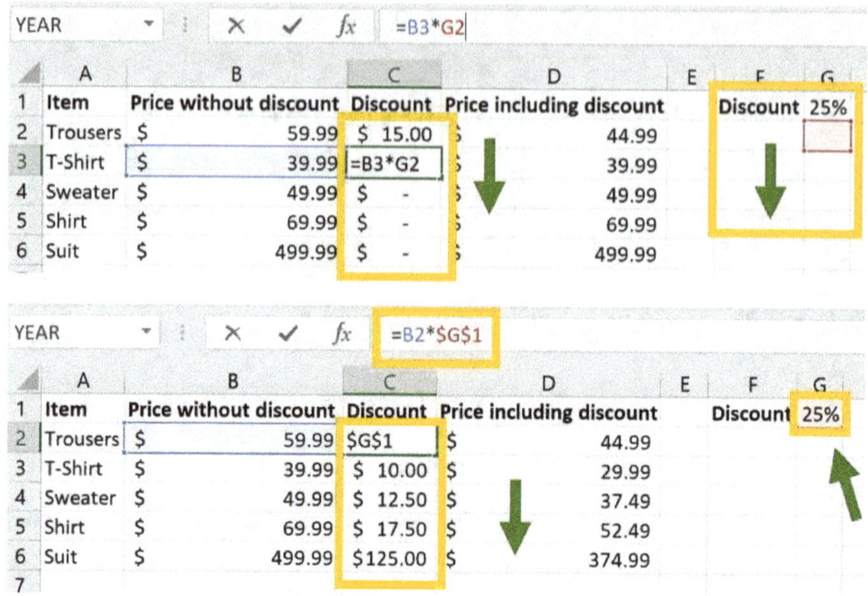

Figure 48: Relative cell reference (top) and absolute cell reference (bottom)

Furthermore, the following relationships apply:

If you place a "$" character only in front of the letter, but not in front of the number, i.e., writing "$A1", only the **column of the cell reference always remains unchanged,** but the row does not. On the other hand, if you write "A$1" – you can guess it – the column can change, but the **row remains fixed**.

Note: *If you want to display a formula of a cell with its function arguments (as in Figure 48; bottom), simply double-click on the cell.*

6.2 Function Library, Define Names & Formula Evaluation

Let us first take a look at the sections of "Formulas". In *Fig. 49* you will find the option "Insert function" (green arrow) on the far left. By clicking on it, a pop-up window with a search and selection tool for functions opens. It is best to use "Insert function" whenever you are not sure which function you need or how it has to be structured. When you click on "OK", another pop-up window "Function arguments" appears, which helps you to select the correct function components.

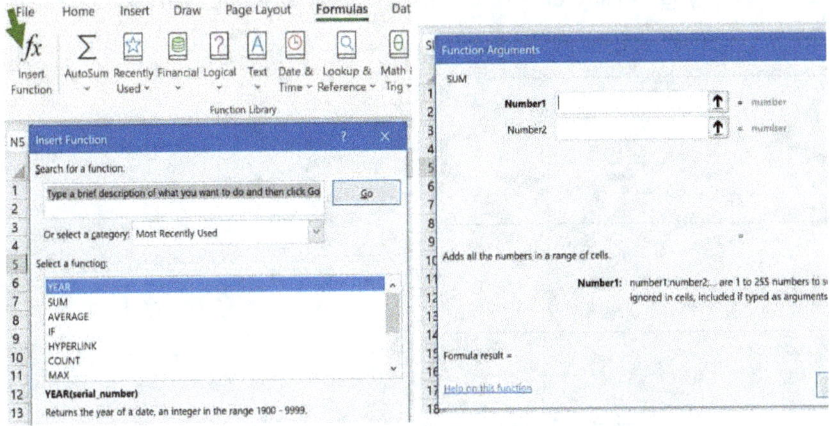

Figure 49: Insert Function (left) and Function Arguments (right)

In the area next to it, you will find often used functions such as "Sum", "Average" or "Count Numbers" (*Fig. 50*).

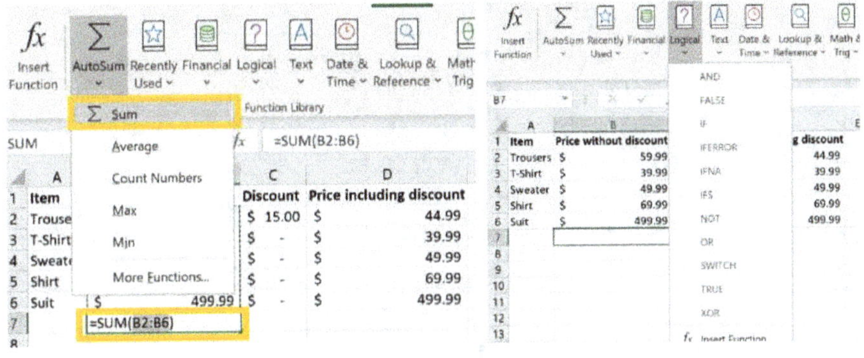

Figure 50: Standard functions and logical operators

Additionally, some categories that give an overview of possible functions. For example, the category "Recently used" or "Logical". How logical operators are used is explained in the next chapter.

If you move further to the right, you will come across "Define names" (*Fig. 51*; right section). Here, you can assign a name to a cell or a whole cell range in Excel. Alternatively, you can also enter the name in the small name field (*Fig. 52*; top left) as mentioned at the beginning of the book.

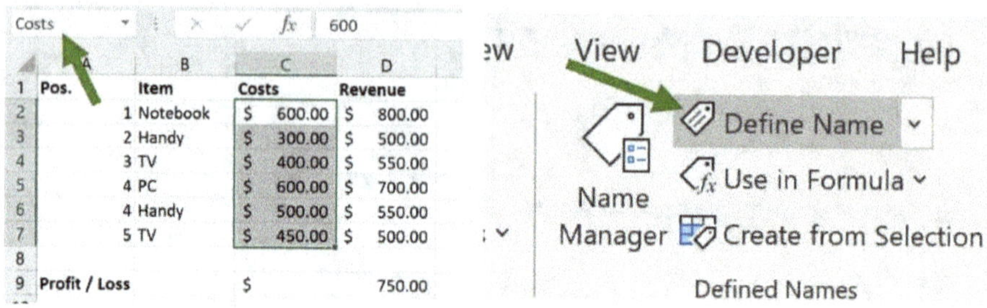

Figure 51: Define names for cells or cell ranges

With the name manager, you can manage the name assignments in your Excel worksheet and insert them with "Use in formula".

	Pos.	Item	Costs	Revenue	
SUM				=SUM(Revenue)-SUM(Costs)	
1	Pos.	Item	Costs	Revenue	
2		1 Notebook	$ 600.00	$ 800.00	
3		2 Handy	$ 300.00	$ 500.00	
4		3 TV	$ 400.00	$ 550.00	
5		4 PC	$ 600.00	$ 700.00	
6		4 Handy	$ 500.00	$ 550.00	
7		5 TV	$ 450.00	$ 500.00	
8					
9	Profit / Loss		Costs)		

Figure 52: Fill functions with "names" instead of cell references

For example, you can create a revenue-surplus account as shown in *Figure 52*. Instead of numbers or cell ranges, simply put the assigned names in the formula "**=SUM**". This function offers a great advantage if you want to present a calculation in a clear and comprehensible way. If you would like to display your cell references clearly structured, use the function "Trace Precedents" or "... Dependents" (see *Fig. 53*; top). Cell references are now indicated by arrows. Also, in *Fig. 53* (bottom) the function "Show formulas" is presented. With this command, you can display all formulas in the worksheet and thus check them more easily (very helpful if you have countless formulas).

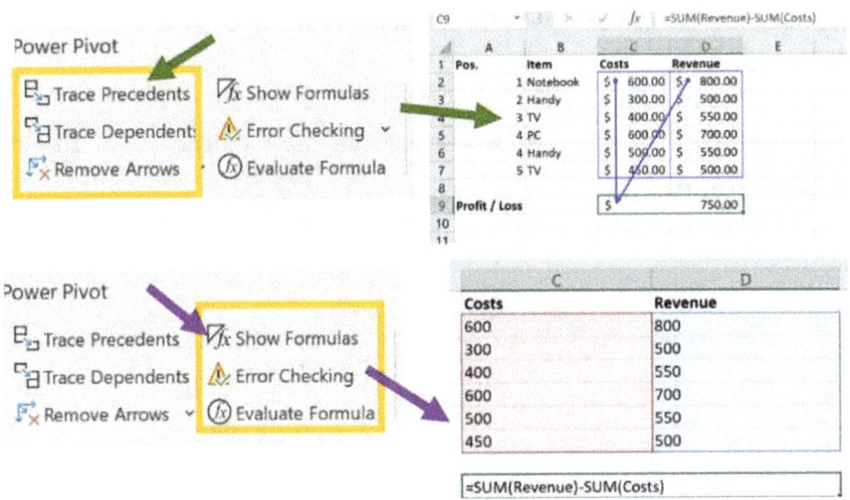

Figure 53: Formula Evaluation using "Trace Precedents" and "Show Formulas"

In *Fig. 54* there are two more very helpful functions for understanding calculation steps and finding bugs.

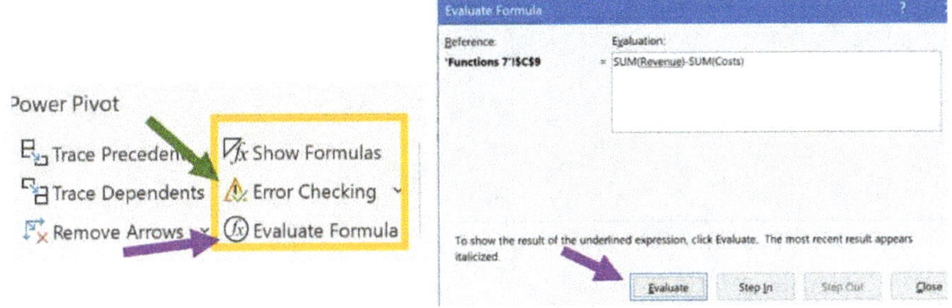

Figure 54: "Error Checking" (green) and "Evaluate Formula" (purple)

Click on a cell that contains a formula and in the pop-up window (that appears when clicking on "Evaluate Formula"; purple arrows in *Fig. 54*) click on "Evaluate" several times in a row. You will notice that the individual calculation steps are displayed in the evaluation field in the upper area. The "Error Checking" function (green arrow) also helps you to correct a formula bug. The "monitoring window" to the right will help you if you need to keep an eye on a calculated value while you perform other calculations that have an influence on this value.

Finally, you will find the functions "Calculation Options", "Calculate Now" or "Calculate Sheet" in the "Formulas" menu on the far right. These are self-explanatory by their respective names.

6.3 Basic Formulas & Important Functions

In Excel, you can choose from several hundred functions to perform calculations. We will content ourselves with the most important ones for now. The procedure remains the same: you select the cell in which you want the result of the calculation and type "=" in the function line followed by the function in CAPITAL LETTERS, followed by brackets with the function arguments.

The basic arithmetic operations in Excel are written as follows:

Addition: z.B. "=A1+B1",

Subtraction: z.B. "=A1-B1",

Multiplication: z.B. "=A1*B1",

Division: z.B. "=A1/B1"

If you have several summands, just write **"=SUM(A1:A6)"**. This gives the following summation: A1+A2+A3+A4+A5+A6. If there are various factors, you write analogously: **"=PRODUCT(A1:A6)"**.

"=SUMIF(range;criteria;sum_range)" sums up everything in the selected sum_range if a certain criteria in another range is fulfilled. **"COUNTIF"(range;criteria)** works similar. With this, you can find out how often a criterion exists in a certain range. Take a look at the example in *Fig. 55*.

YEAR		× ✓	fx	=COUNTIF(B2:D8;50)	
	A	**B**	**C**	**D**	**E**
1	**Student**	**Math points**	**Language points**	**Art points**	**Average**
2	Thomas	10	30	20	20
3	Klaus	20	20	30	23.3
4	Frieda	10	10	20	13.3
5	Thorsten	30	50	40	40.0
6	Sven	20	30	50	33.3
7	Claudia	50	20	10	26.7
8	Lisa	20	10	20	16.7
9					
10	**How often?**	**50 points**	**20 points**	**10 points**	
11		D8;50)			

Figure 55: How often was a particular score given?

To make a sort of logical test before an action, use this function: "**=IF(**logical_test**;**value_if_true**;**value_if_false**)**".

A shop that offers a discount of -10% from a total purchase value greater than $ 500 is shown in the example in *Fig. 56*. In this case, the logical test is "D8>500", i.e., the total purchase value (corresponds to cell D8) is checked. Value_if_true equals cell "F2" and Value_if_false should return a "0" for "no discount".

YEAR		× ✓	fx	=IF(D8>500;F2;0)			
	A	**B**	**C**	**D**	**E**	**F**	**G** H
1	**Quantity**	**Item**	**Unit Price**	**Total Price**		**Discount for purchase value over $500**	
2	2	Trousers	$ 59.99	$ 119.98		-10%	
3	4	T-Shirt	$ 39.99	$ 159.96			
4	3	Sweater	$ 49.99	$ 149.97			
5	2	Shirt	$ 69.99	$ 139.98			
6	1	Suit	$ 499.99	$ 499.99			
7							
8			Subtotal	1,069.88 €			
9			Discount	F2;0)			
10			minus	- 106.99 €			
11			Total	962.89 €			

Figure 56: Discount of -10% for purchase value greater than $ 500 (IF-function)

If you have data where several pieces of information are combined in one cell, e.g., due to an import error, you can use the function "**=MID(text;start_num;num_chars)**" (*Abb. 57*).

B2			fx	=MID(A2;1;5)

	A	B	C	D
1	**imported data**	**Postal Code**		
2	80339 Munich	80339	1	
3	70173 Stuttgart	70173	2	
4	10115 Berlin	10115	3	

Figure 57: Split data with "=MID"

As can be seen in *Fig. 57*, for example, we only want to extract the postal code from a data set. Text represents the range in which our data is located (i.e., the cells in column A). The postal code starts at the very beginning, i.e., start_num = 1 and is 5 characters long, i.e., num_chars = 5. *Note: As you may have noticed, this procedure only works if the data has an identical number of characters (also see 7.3 Data Tools)*

For the next function, imagine the following situation: You need to transfer data from one table to another – almost identical – one. The problem is that the arrangement of the data does not match. This issue can be solved by using the function "=Lookup" or in this case, "=VLookup". Without this function, you would have to search for the individual data with great effort and transfer the individual values manually. First, let's take a look at the example in *Fig. 58*.

| AR | ▼ | : | × | ✓ | f_x | =VLOOKUP(A2;$E$2:$F$5;2;FALSE) |

VLOOKUP(**lookup_value**; table_array; col_index_num; [range_lookup])

A	B	C		Order no.	Total	Quantity
Order no.	Customer	Total				
19273	Maier	A2;$E$2:	2	28292	49.99	1
29732	Huber	39.99		19273	99.98	2
28292	Müller	49.99		29732	39.99	3
22234	Schmidt	299.99		22234	299.99	4

Figure 58: "=VLookup"

We have two table areas. The task consists of transferring data from the right table, which only contains order numbers and purchase values, to the table on the left-hand side (in *Fig. 58*). This has already been done by "=VLookup".) As the order numbers are not listed parallel, they would have to be searched for and entered manually if we would not use a function.

"**=VLookup(lookup_value;table_array;col_index_num;range_lookup)**" uses the lookup value to specify the element to be searched for (we search for the respective order number). Table array indicates the range to be searched in (note the absolute cell references "$" to be able to perform an auto-complete). Col_index_num means, in which column the values that we need are located (in this case, the purchase value is in column 2 of the selected range) and at range_lookup you can choose between "True" or "False". "True" would mean that there is only an approximate match between search term and value. Therefore, we need "False", which implies an exact match.

Besides "=Lookup" and "=**V**Lookup" there is also "=**H**Lookup". Do not get confused, the only difference is that "=HLookup" refers to **rows** and "=VLookup" to **columns**. "=Lookup(lookup_value;array)" by itself always selects the last value in a row/column. This means that in our example, the function "=Lookup" would have been sufficient, since the searched value (purchase value) is in the last column (the table on the right only consists of 2 columns, so the purchase value is the "last" column). The prefixes "**V**" or "**H**" are used if you need the value of a column/row from several columns or rows. Just try all three versions!

If several conditions are to be linked simultaneously, so-called logical operators must be used. This sounds more complicated than it seems because in Excel, it is only about terms like "and" and "or". In *Figure 59*, for example, we want to match two conditions in a table. We look for furniture that has the color "natural" and costs less than $ 100. If both conditions are met, we want "ok" to be displayed. Otherwise, "not ok". For this, we use "=IF" and "AND".

| YEAR | ▾ | ⋮ | ✕ | ✓ | *fx* | =IF(AND(B2="natural";(C2<100));"ok";"not ok") |

	A	B	C	D	E	F	G
1	Item	Color	Price			ok / not ok	
2	Picture frame	blue	20			ok")	
3	Table	natural	150			not ok	
4	Chair	natural	50			ok	
5	Picture frame	yellow	80			not ok	
6	Chair	brown	55			not ok	
7	Table	black	90			not ok	

Figure 59: Multi-conditional logical test

Alternatively, as in *Fig. 60*, we would also accept that the furniture is brown. We implement this with "OR".

| \R | ▾ | ⋮ | ✕ | ✓ | *fx* | =IF(AND(OR(B2="natural";B2="brown");(C2<100));"ok";"not ok") |

A	B	C	D	E	F	G	H
Item	Color	Price			ok / not ok		
Picture frame	blue	20			ok")		
Table	natural	150			not ok		
Chair	natural	50			ok		
Picture frame	yellow	80			not ok		
Chair	brown	55			ok		
Table	black	90			not ok		

Figure 60: Linking "=IF"-conditions with "=AND" and "=OR"

If you nest functions like here, you can do this without "=" before "AND" or "OR". But if you use these operators independently, you need the "=" characters.

In the next chapter, you will find another and somewhat more complicated function. We are going to create an Excel spreadsheet containing a sophisticated search function. But before we do that, we will discuss "Filter" and "Conditional Formatting" in more detail.

*Note: Another important function, called =SUMPRODUCT(array 1;array2) is presented in chapter **9 Developer** using an example.*

7 Data

7.1 Get/Transform Data and Queries & Connections

In the left of the ribbon area "Data" you can insert data from external sources and, if necessary, transform them into a preferred format. Imagine, for example, that you receive data in a text file separated by semicolons (see *Fig. 61*; left) and want to transfer them into your Excel sheet.

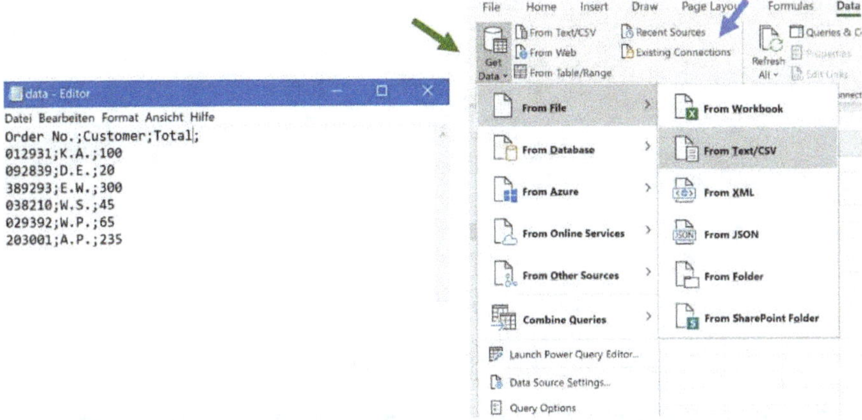

Figure 61: Insert data from an external source into Excel

As you can see in *Figure 61*, you can import data from many different sources (green arrow). You can also insert data from often used source formats using the small shortcuts (blue arrow).

After you have selected a file by clicking on "from Text/CSV" (pop-up window opens), another pop-up window as shown in *Fig. 62* will appear, where you can set the "File Origin", the "Delimiter" of the original file and the "Data Type Detection" (framed in orange). In our example, everything should have been detected automatically. Then you can "load" or "transform" the data in Excel (blue arrows). By "Loading" the files will be accepted as in the pre-view field (green arrow). "Transform" opens the Power Query Editor (see *Fig. 63*), with which you can/could edit the data according to your needs.

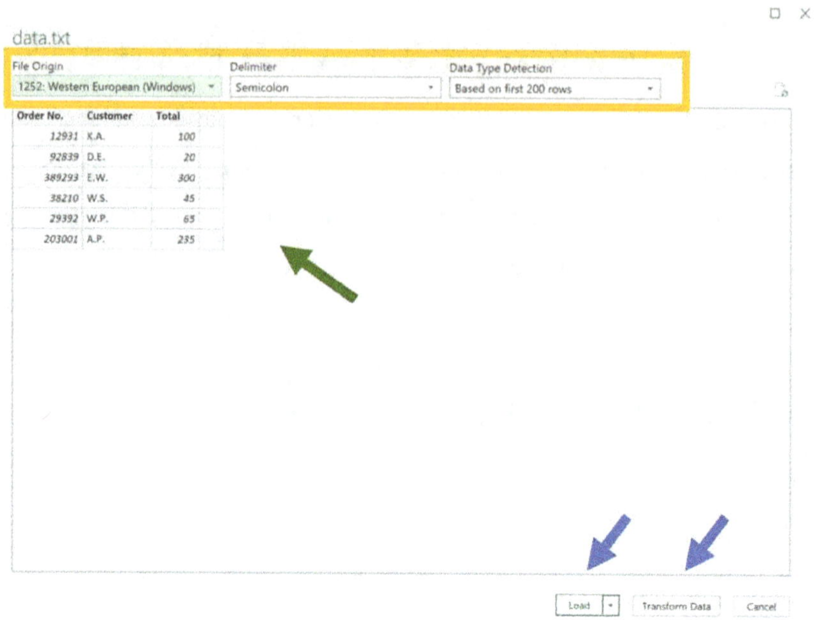

Figure 62: Data import

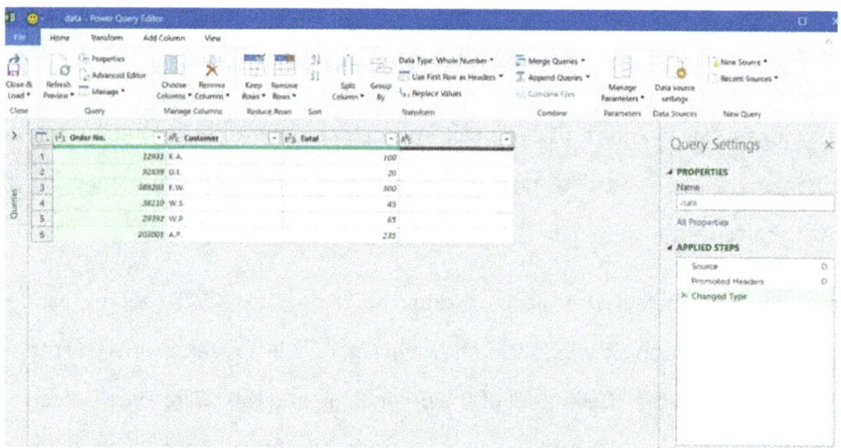

Figure 63: Power Query Editor for further editing before data import

Try the various functions. Essentially, in this editor you can add or remove columns or rows and make several adjustments to format and data.

In the next example, we will insert data from the web. The benefit of that is, that this "live" data can be updated. This is useful, for example, if we need a currency conversion of item prices as in *Fig. 64*. The exchange rate fluctuates over time and would therefore have to be laboriously researched and pasted into the sheet every day.

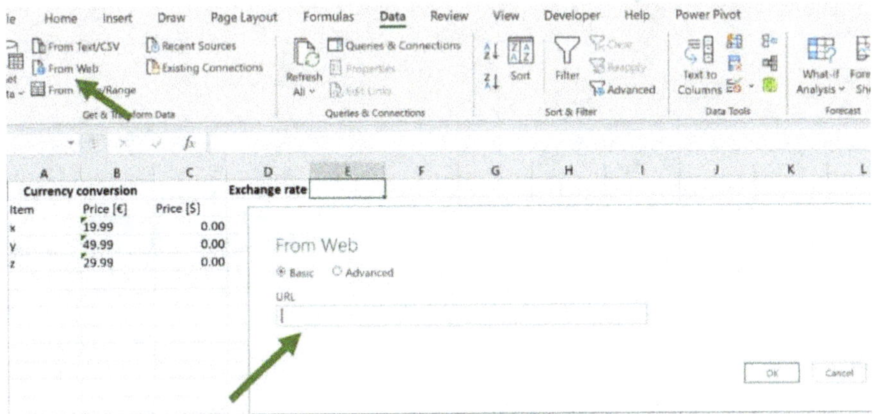

Figure 64: Import data from the web (exchange rate)

Find a website that provides exchange rates, such as https://markets.ft.com/data/currencies/tearsheet/summary?s=EURUSD and enter it as shown in *Fig. 63* (green arrow). Then choose "OK" and confirm the next pop-up window with "Connect".

In the following window, as shown in *Fig. 65.1*, select e.g., "Table 0" in the left area (green arrow) and import the data with "Load".

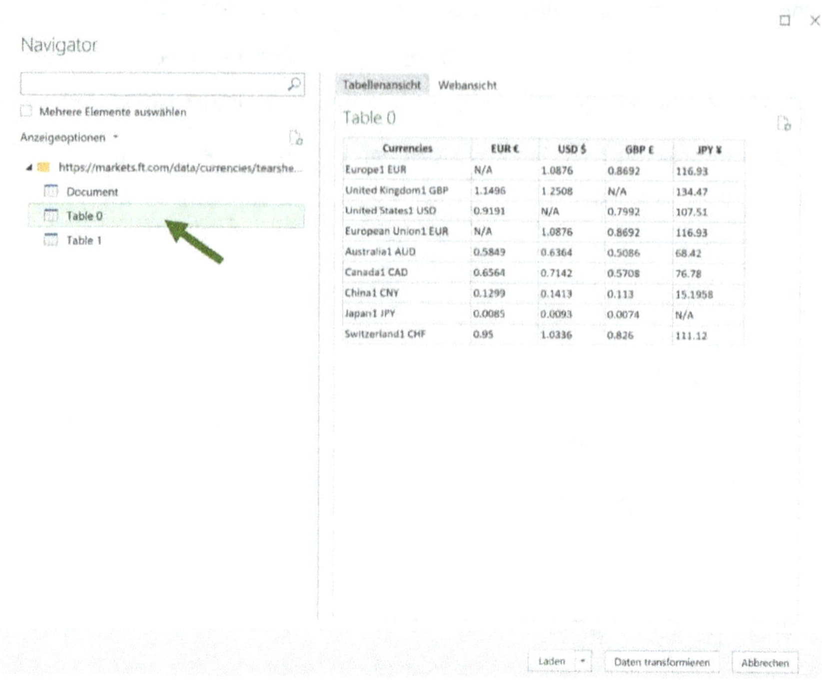

Figure 65.1: "Navigator" pop-up window for data selection

The exchange rates listed are then inserted in a new sheet (*Fig. 65.2*):

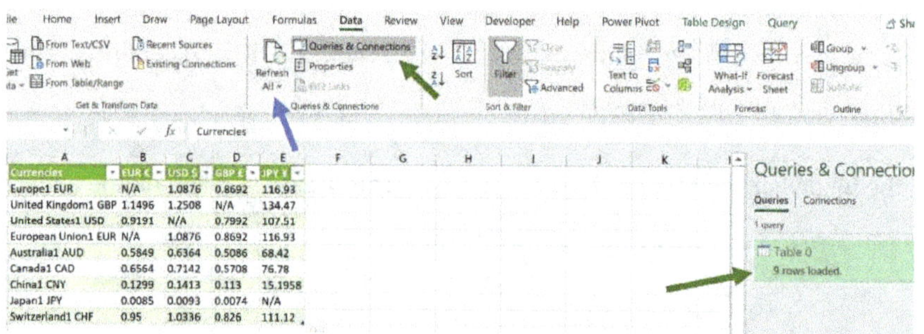

Figure 65.2: "Refresh all" and "Queries & Connections" for data updating

In the section "Data" (*Fig. 65.2*; top) you can open an area (opens on the right) where you can manage connections to content (green arrows). By clicking on the button "Update all" (blue arrow), the content is refreshed automatically if an internet connection is available and firewall permission is granted.

Finally, make a link to the cell "Exchange rate" in your spreadsheet as follows: Write "=" in the cell where you need the exchange rate, and then switch to the sheet with the exchange rate table. Now select the cell containing the exchange rate as shown in *Figure 66* and confirm by clicking on "Enter".

C2			✗	✓	*fx*	='Currency Conv.'!C2

	A	B	C	D	E
1	Currencies	EUR €	USD $	GBP £	JPY ¥
2	Europe1 EUR	N/A	1.0876	0.8692	116.93
3	United Kingdom1 GBP	1.1496	1.2508	N/A	134.47
4	United States1 USD	0.9191	N/A	0.7992	107.51
5	European Union1 EUR	N/A	1.0876	0.8692	116.93
6	Australia1 AUD	0.5849	0.6364	0.5086	68.42
7	Canada1 CAD	0.6564	0.7142	0.5708	76.78
8	China1 CNY	0.1299	0.1413	0.113	15.1958
9	Japan1 JPY	0.0085	0.0093	0.0074	N/A
10	Switzerland1 CHF	0.95	1.0336	0.826	111.12

Figure 66: Make a cell reference to another worksheet

7.2 Filter

You already know the feature "Sort" from **Chapter 2.6**. There is not much more to say here, except that you can also sort by color, as you will see in the following. But at first, let's move on to the feature "Filter". After selecting a data range as shown in *Fig. 67*, click on "Filter" (green arrow; top) and little drop-down menus will appear in the first row of a data range (green arrow; center). If you select them, you can choose which data should be filtered. You can also apply a "Text filter" or "Custom filter..." (orange arrow) and set some advanced filtering criteria (purple arrow).

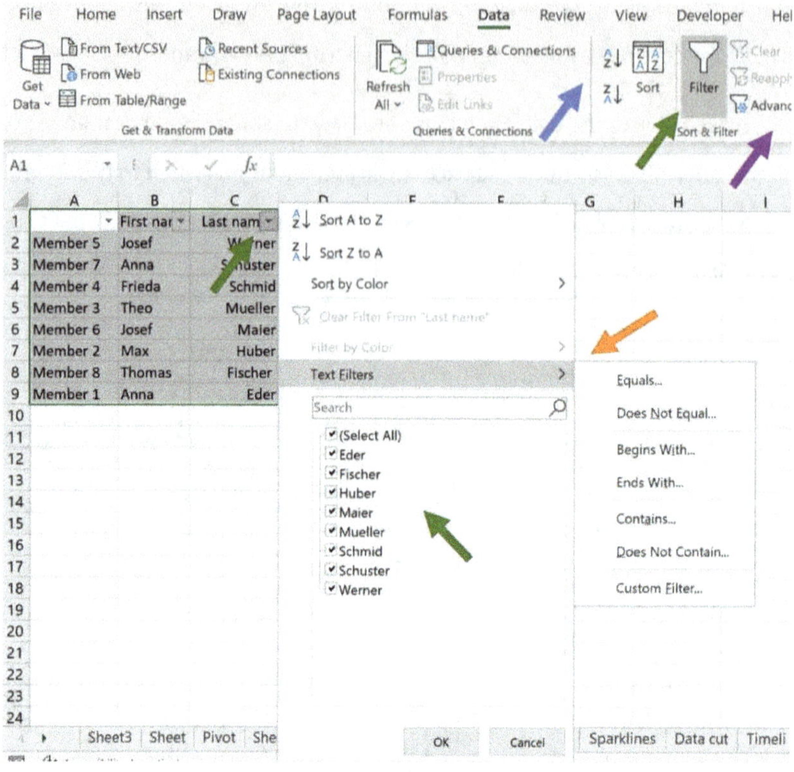

Figure 67: "Sort" and "Filter"

But how do you use a text filter or a custom filter? Let's take a look at *Figure 68*. In this example, we want to create a filter that will only show us names containing the letter "i" in the column "Last Name". We select "Text Filters" → "Contains..." and enter the letter "i" in the pop-up window "Custom AutoFilter". After confirming, we get back the table filtered by last names containing the letter "i". The small filter symbol (framed in red) indicates that a filter is active in this column. You can remove the filter by clicking on this symbol and simply select "Clear filter ...". Also try a second condition, linked with "Begins with..." or "Ends with..." and other filters like "Equals..." or "Does not Equal...". In addition, you can use a date filter in the column "Birthday" instead of a text filter. The procedure is identical, just try it!

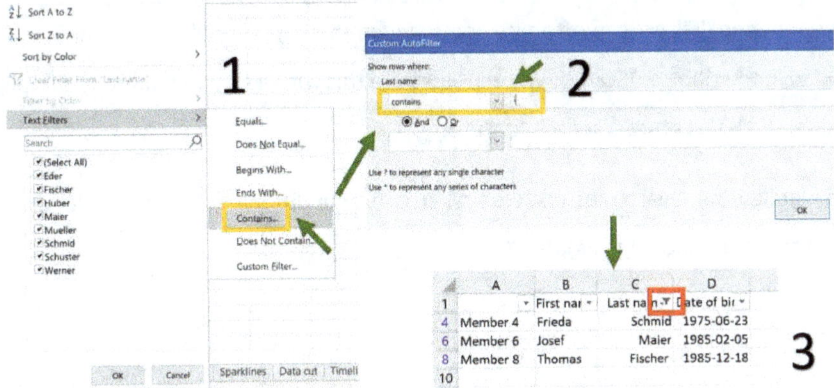

Figure 68: Creating a "Contains..." Filter operation

An "Advanced Filter" works as shown in *Fig. 69*. We can use this function to filter according to several criteria, which we define separately (framed in green).

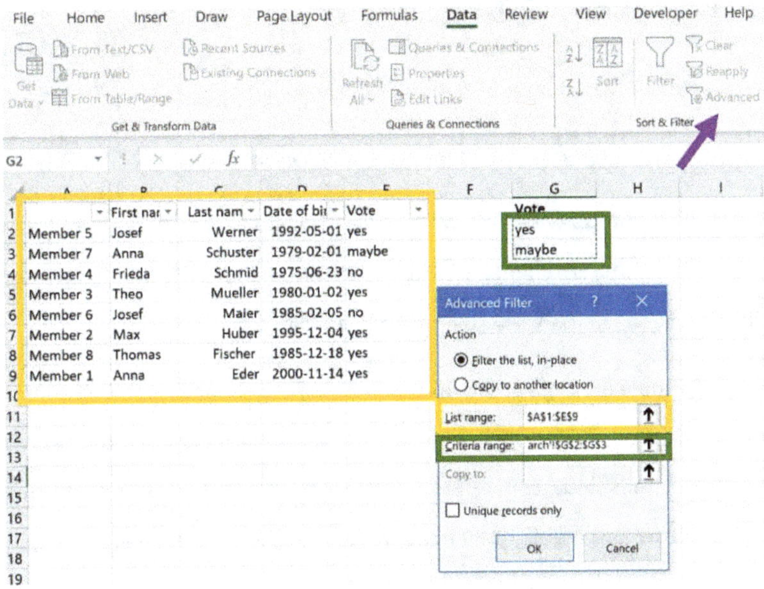

Figure 69: "Advanced Filter": Filtering by criteria range

Select the list range (framed in orange) and the criteria range (framed in green) and confirm. You will then see all those who voted with "yes" and "maybe". However, filtering becomes more useful if you filter by multiple criteria.

The function "Filter" can often be combined with "Conditional Formatting" (to be found in the ribbon: "Start"). We will illustrate this with a somewhat more complex example - let's create a search feature.

To highlight our search results, we first create a conditional formatting rule for the data range, as shown in *Figure 70*.

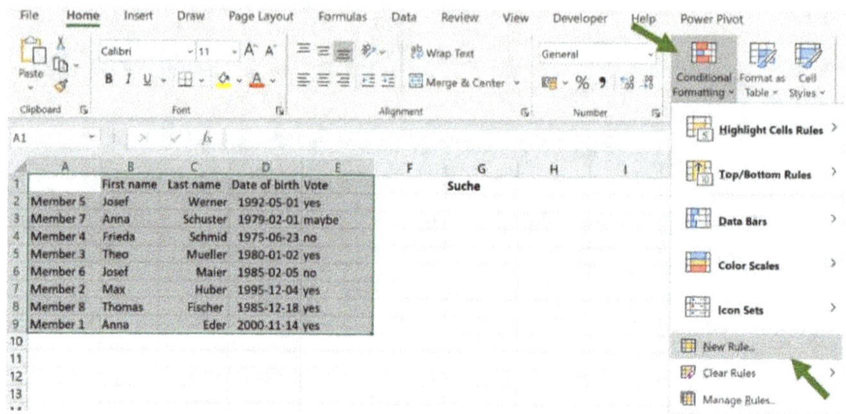

Figure 70: Creating a new conditional formatting rule

In the following pop-up window, "New Formatting Rule". (Fig. 71) we select "Use a formula to determine..." and enter the following formula: **=AND(ISTEXT($H$1);FIND($H$1;$A2&$B2&$C2&$D2&$E2))**

When this formula is run, all rows in ranges A through E are selected (relative cell reference starting at "2" because data starts at row 2) that contain the search field term of $H$1 (absolute cell reference). Since we want to search through all columns of a row and highlight all rows, we use "&" as a link between $A2, $B2, ... AND indicates that all subsequent conditions must be met. ISTTEXT is required so that not everything is highlighted if the search field ($H$1) is empty.

Then click on "Format" (blue arrow) so that you can define how the results should be highlighted. In this case, the lines should be filled in, e.g., orange (Fig. 72).

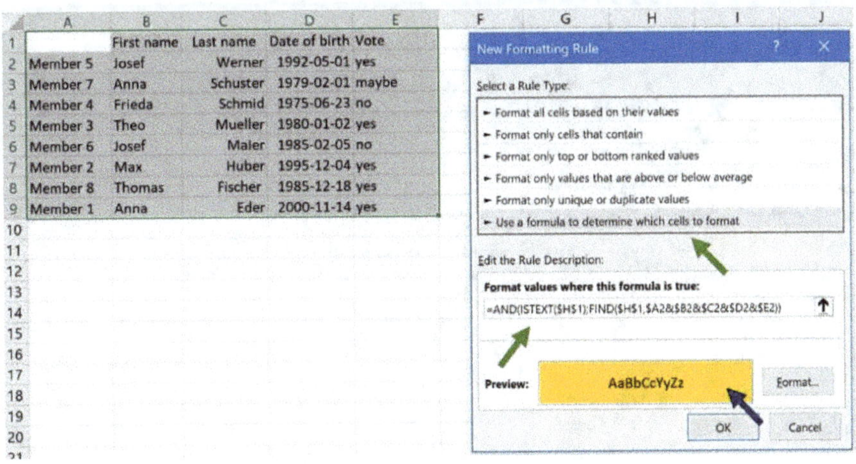

Figure 71: Creating a formatting rule using a formula

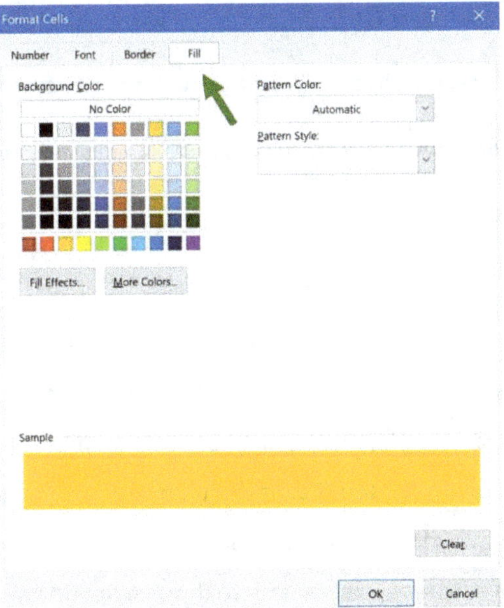

Figure 72: Select formatting for the condition

If you now enter a term in the search field (upper/lower case does not matter & even text fragments can be searched) and press "Enter", the search terms found are highlighted (*Fig. 73*). If you create a filter and select "Filter by color", only the results found will be displayed.

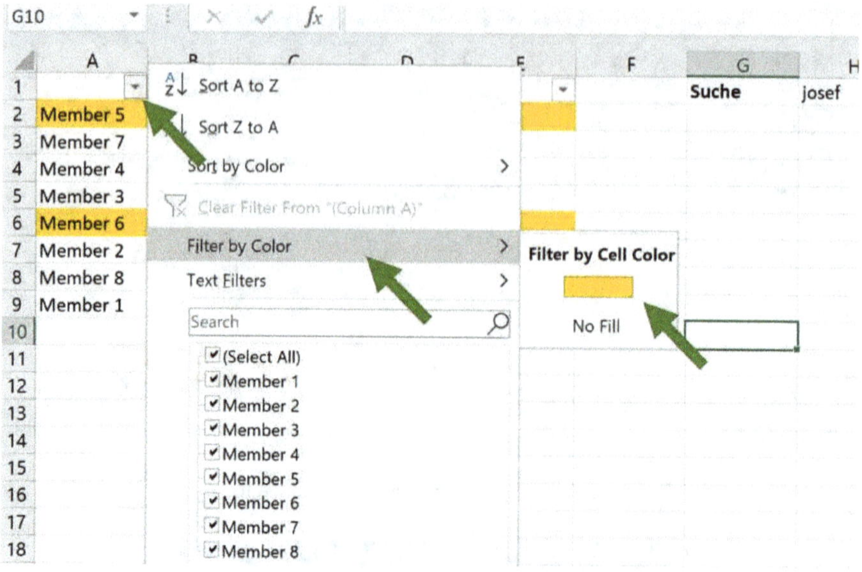

Figure 73: Displayed search results are highlighted in color. Activating a color filter

In Chapter 9 Developer, **we will come back to this example and extend it a bit further.**

7.3 Data Tools

You probably remember the "Postcode" example from *Chapter 6.3 Basic Formulas & Important Functions*. With the help of "Text to Columns", Excel offers us a somewhat simpler and more effective way to solve that problem. To do this, select the data and click on the button "Text to columns" in the section "Data Tools". In the pop-up window, you can choose between "Delimited" and "Fixed width" (depending on the data type, please refer to the description given by Excel). In this case, we select " Delimited". Then click on "Next" (see *Fig. 74*).

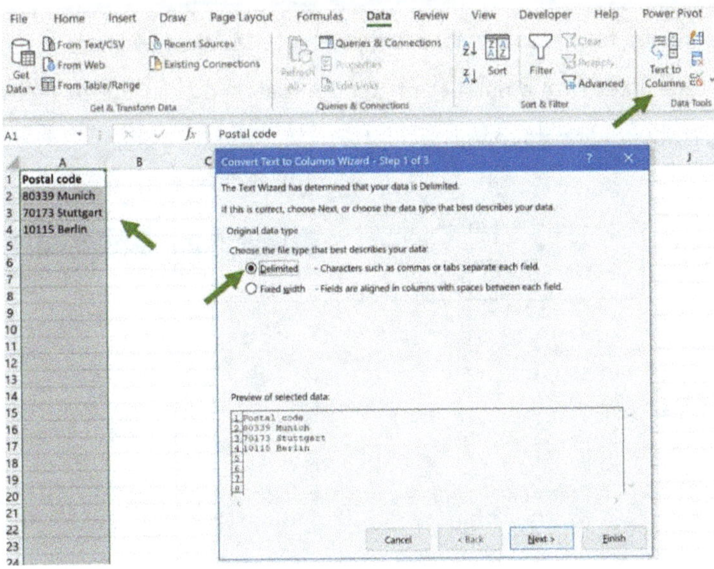

Figure 74: Split text into columns

In the next step of the "Convert Text to Column Wizard", select the separator of the data, in this case "Space" and in the last step the data format, we want "Standard". As a result, you will get a separation of the data after the space character into two separate columns (see *Figure 75*).

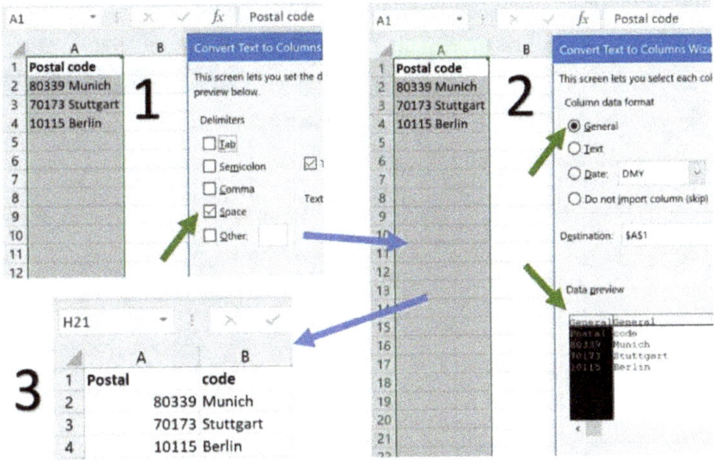

Figure 75: "Text to column wizard" steps 2 & 3 including result

Another helpful feature is provided with "Remove Duplicates" (see *Fig. 76*). If you have a data sheet with a number of identical data, you can use this function to delete all redundant data rows.

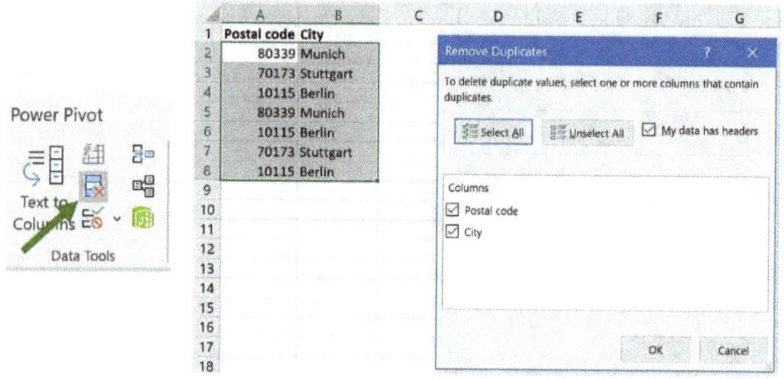

Figure 76: Use "Remove Duplicates" for superfluous data

If you want to equipt cells with drop-down lists instead of allowing all cell entries, you can use "Data Validation". Start as shown in *Figure 77* (green arrow → orange arrow → blue arrow). Select "List" under "Allow" and enter the terms with a "**;**" as separator, e.g., fish;chicken;meat;vegetarian.

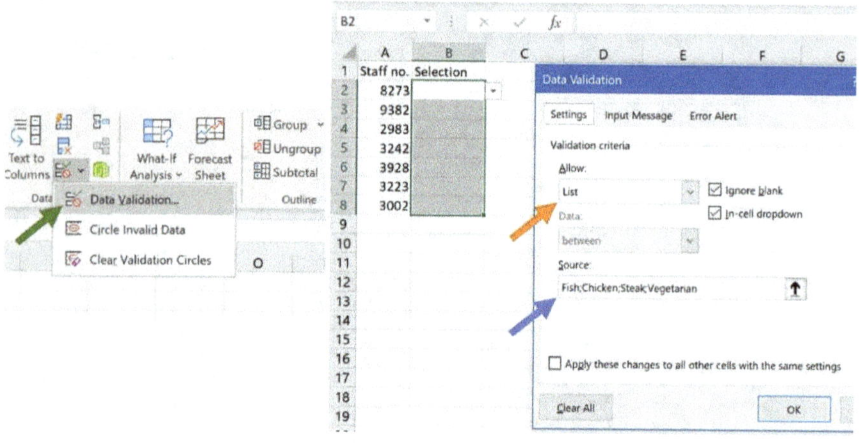

Figure 77: Create data selectors using "Data Validation"

As you will see in *Figure 78*, this allows us to create a drop-down list:

	A	B	C
1	Staff no.	Selection	
2	8273		
3	9382	Fish	
4	2983	Chicken	
5	3242	Steak	
6	3928	Vegetarian	
7	3223		
8	3002		
9			

Figure 78: Selection options in the form of a drop-down list

If you want to display a brief description, e.g., to explain what to do and/or to display an error message if someone tries to enter a different text in the cell, proceed as shown in *Fig. 79* in "Data Validation":

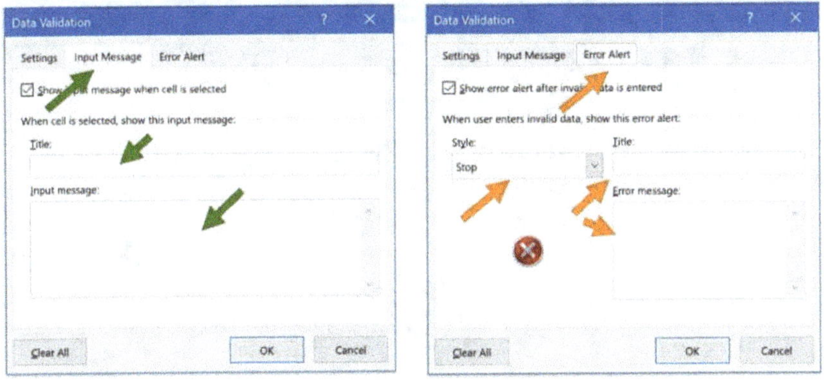

Figure 79: Display input message and/or error message

7.4 What-If Analysis

There are two helpful tools in the drop-down of "What-If Analysis". One is the "Scenario Manager" and the other is "Goal Seek". You can use the Scenario

Manager whenever you want to create different scenarios, such as "Best Case" or "Worst Case". We will take a look at this using the example of a sales forecast.

Let's assume we have the sales figures for the first quarter, and we would like to create a worst case and best-case scenario for the second quarter (framed in orange). Assume that we already know the expenses. Start as in *Fig. 80* and enter your first forecast in cells E2 to G2 (sales April-June).

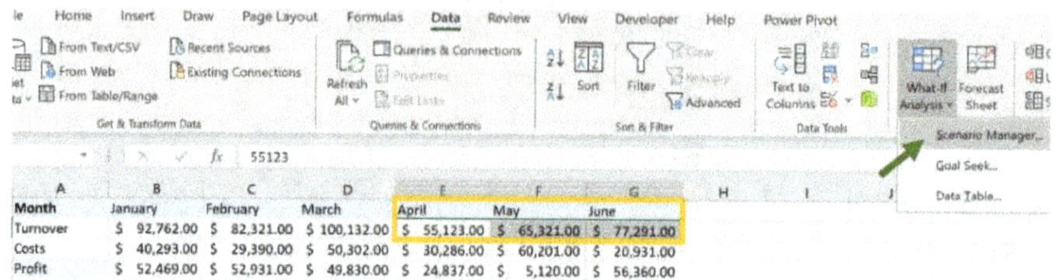

Figure 80: Creating a scenario with "What-If Analysis"

Then select the button "Add" in the pop-up window "Scenario Manager". In this window, you can manage the created scenarios.

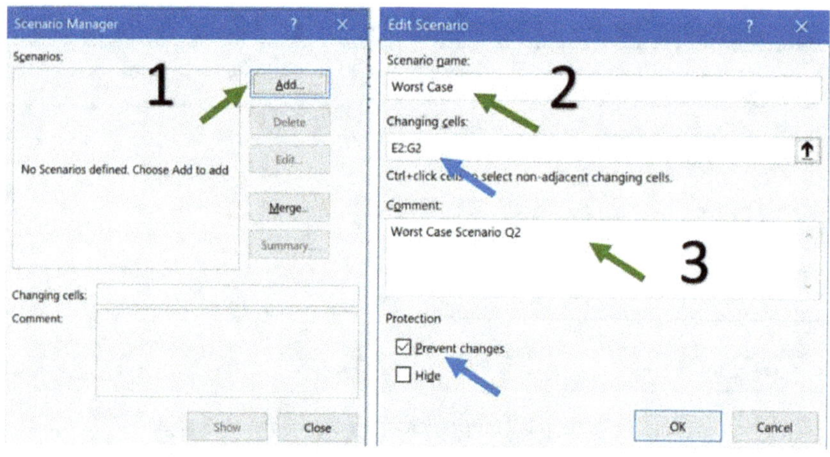

Figure 81: Creating the worst-case scenario

In the next window, you enter a name and — if you want to — a comment for the scenario (green arrows). In the area of the blue arrows, you can change the cell range or (de)activate a protection against changes. Confirm with "OK" and a window named "Scenario values" will appear (*Fig. 82*), where you can enter values or just review them.

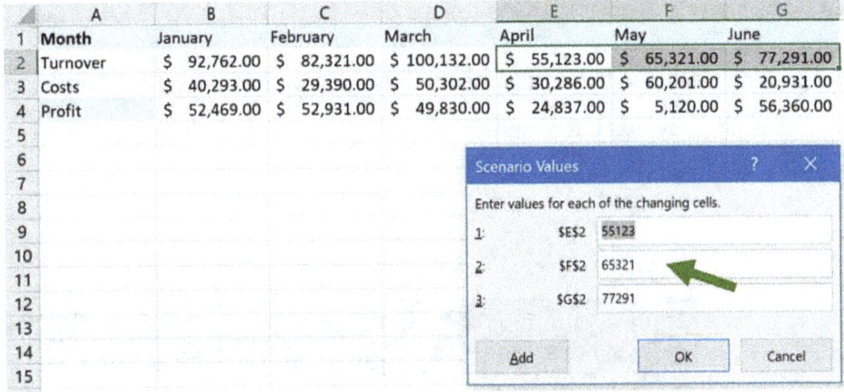

Figure 82: Enter or check scenario values

Confirm with "OK". The "Scenario Manager" appears. Then create a best-case scenario using the same procedure, and you will get a situation as shown in *Fig. 83* (left side).

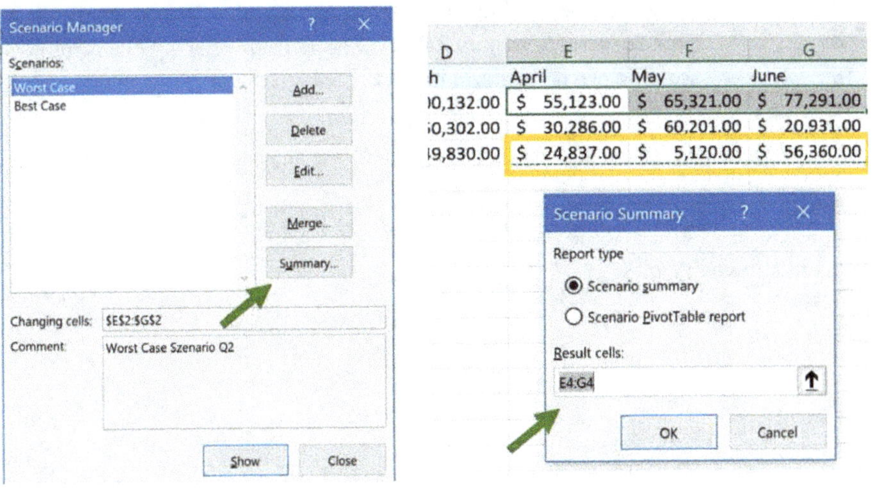

Figure 83: "Scenario Manager" with scenarios (left side). Create Summary (right side)

With a click on "Summary" you can automatically create a scenario summary. For the report, you select – as shown in *Fig. 83* (right side) – the cells that interest you in your analysis. In our case, this would be the profit of the respective months, i.e., "E4:G4" (framed in orange).

In *Fig. 84* you can see the scenario summary for a profit forecast for the second quarter created by Excel. It shows the current situation as well as the worst-case and best-case scenario.

		Current Values:	Worst Case	Best Case
Scenario Summary				
Changing Cells:				
	$E$2	$ 55,123.00	$ 55,123.00	$ 104,123.00
	$F$2	$ 65,321.00	$ 65,321.00	$ 115,321.00
	$G$2	$ 77,291.00	$ 77,291.00	$ 110,291.00
Result Cells:				
	$E$4	$ 24,837.00	$ 24,837.00	$ 73,837.00
	$F$4	$ 5,120.00	$ 5,120.00	$ 55,120.00
	$G$4	$ 56,360.00	$ 56,360.00	$ 89,360.00

Notes: Current Values column represents values of changing cells at time Scenario Summary Report was created. Changing cells for each scenario are highlighted in gray.

Figure 84: Scenario Summary showing worst-case and best-case scenarios

A scenario can also be displayed in a table with the help of "Data table". To do this, start as shown in *Fig. 85*:

	A	B	C	D	E	F	G	H	I
	Unit Price	49.99							
	Surcharge (fixed)	20%							
	Quantity	5							
	Profit	299.94							
							Unit Price		
			299.94	29.99	34.95	39.99	44.95	49.99	59.99
		Q	1						
		u	5						
		a	20						
		n	50						
		t	100						
		i	500						
		t							
		y							

Figure 85: Preparations for "Data table"

*Note: The formula for calculating the profit in cell **B4** is: =(B1+B1*B2)*B3 In cell **C6** you enter a link to the cell containing the profit, i.e., =B4.*

We can now let Excel complete the table, i.e., calculate the profit for each combination of item price and quantity in our table. To do this, mark the table area and start "Data Table" within the drop-down of "What-If Analysis". Then select the data for the row and column (see *Figure 86*). For "Row" select the item price (**$B$1**, blue arrow) and for the column the quantity (**$B$3**, green arrow). Why? Because in our table, the rows contain the item prices and the columns contain the quantities (framed in orange and blue).

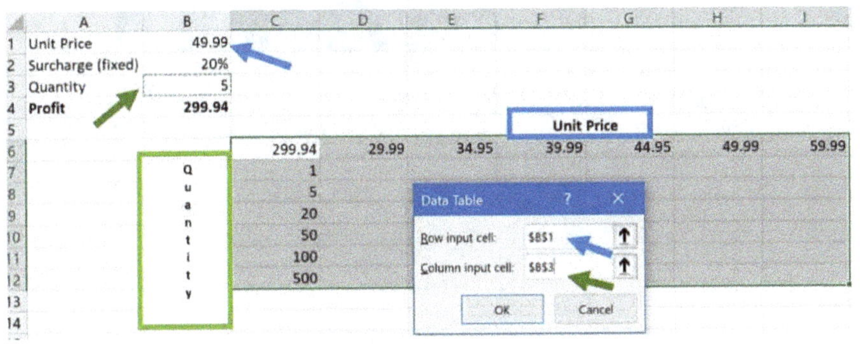

Figure 86: Specify input cells for the data table

As a result, you will receive the calculated profit for each specified combination of item price and item quantity:

	Unit Price					
299.94	29.99	34.95	39.99	44.95	49.99	59.99
1	35.988	41.94	47.988	53.94	59.988	71.988
5	179.94	209.7	239.94	269.7	299.94	359.94
20	719.76	838.8	959.76	1078.8	1199.76	1439.76
50	1799.4	2097	2399.4	2697	2999.4	3599.4
100	3598.8	4194	4798.8	5394	5998.8	7198.8
500	17994	20970	23994	26970	29994	35994

Figure 87: Completed data table with profit for each combination

The last function of the "What-If Analysis" drop-down is "Goal seek". This feature allows us to define a target that we want to achieve by varying a specific value. For example, we would like to achieve a certain profit and let the price of the item be calculated. Besides using an equation, this also works with "Goal seek" in the form of a mathematical iteration. After opening "Goal seek", first determine the necessary parameters as shown in *Fig. 88*.

Figure 88: Set parameters for "Goal seek"

With a click on "OK", Excel performs an iteration to determine the required item price, which gives us a profit of $ 1000 by selling a fixed quantity with surcharge (see *Fig. 89*).

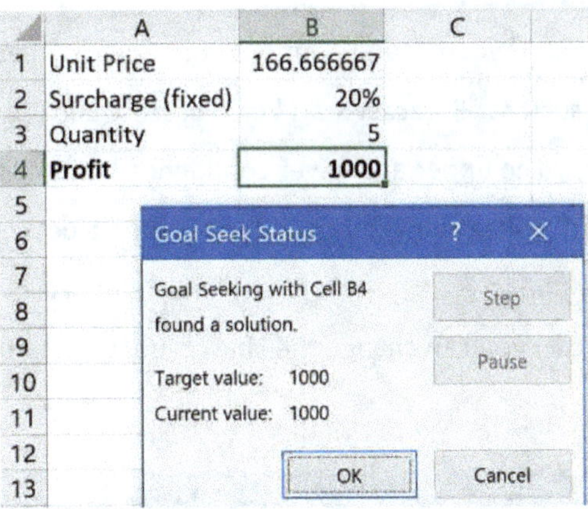

Figure 89: Result of "Goal seek"

7.5 Forecast Worksheet

To visualize a forecast, Excel offers a real eye-catcher with its tool "Forecast Worksheet". Imagine you have to enter profit figures every week and want to visualize the trend for the next weeks in a graphical way. Create a table like in *Fig. 90*, mark the data range and select "Forecast Worksheet" and you will get the following:

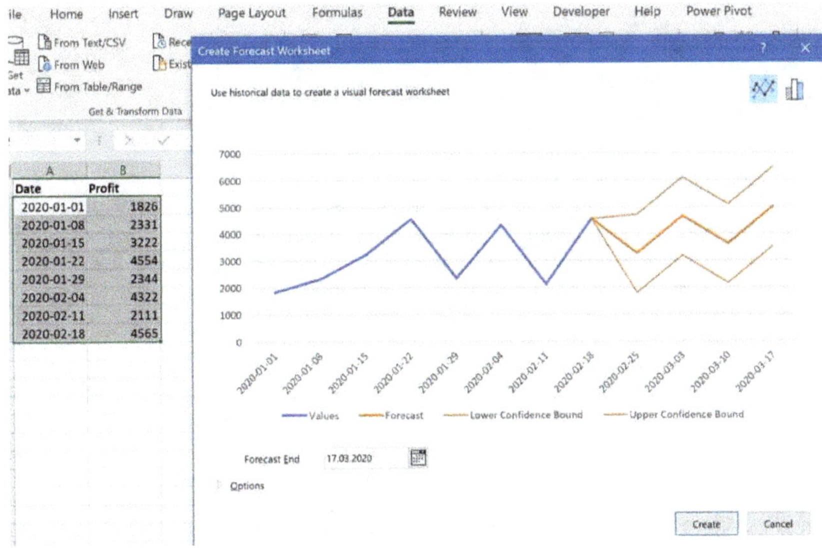

Figure 90: Forecast worksheet for profit evaluation

Take a look at *Fig. 91*. If you expand "Options" (green arrow) as shown here, you can make settings such as "Forecast Start" or "Forecast End" (orange arrows) and some other settings. The upper and lower confidence limits of the worksheet tell you that there is a 95% (settings) probability that the values will be in the range between the upper and lower orange forecast lines. With a click on the little chart symbol (purple arrow) you can change the chart type. Choose between line chart and bar chart.

Figure 91: Forecast worksheet settings

After clicking on "Create" you will receive the forecast sheet and the corresponding values:

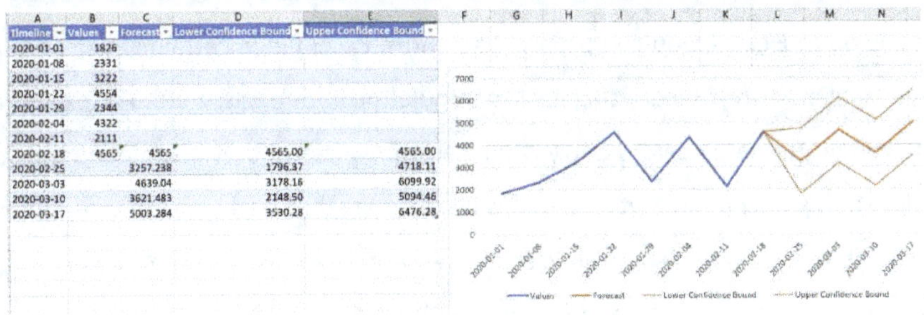

Figure 92: Result: Forecast worksheet and data table

8 Review

In the ribbon area "Review" you can start a "Spelling" or "Accessibility" check (left side of the menu bar), as well as a "Smart Lookup" of terms directly within the Excel worksheet. Accessibility means in this context that the document is optimally formatted, labeled and readable for all persons. Furthermore, "Comments" and "Notes" can be added and edited (see *Fig. 93*).

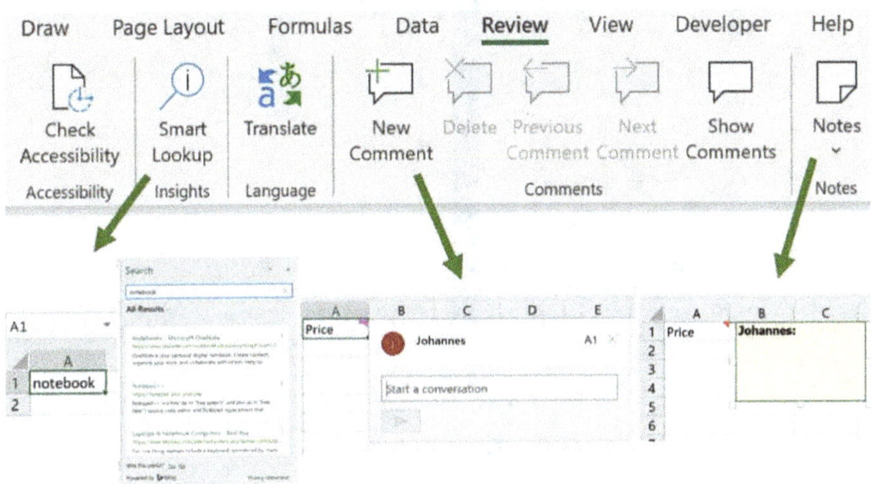

Figure 93: "Smart Lookup", "New comment" and "Notes"

In the right area of the menu bar (Ribbon: "Review") you will find an important function to protect your Excel worksheet.

As shown in *Fig. 94*, you can protect the entire Excel file, a certain sheet or only individual areas or functions against manipulation with a password. For example, you can request a password entry when selecting a cell or only if someone tries to delete a row or column. Determine this by selecting the checkboxes in the window "Protect Sheet". With "Allow all users of this worksheet to" you can also explicitly define ranges in which you allow editing without password entry.

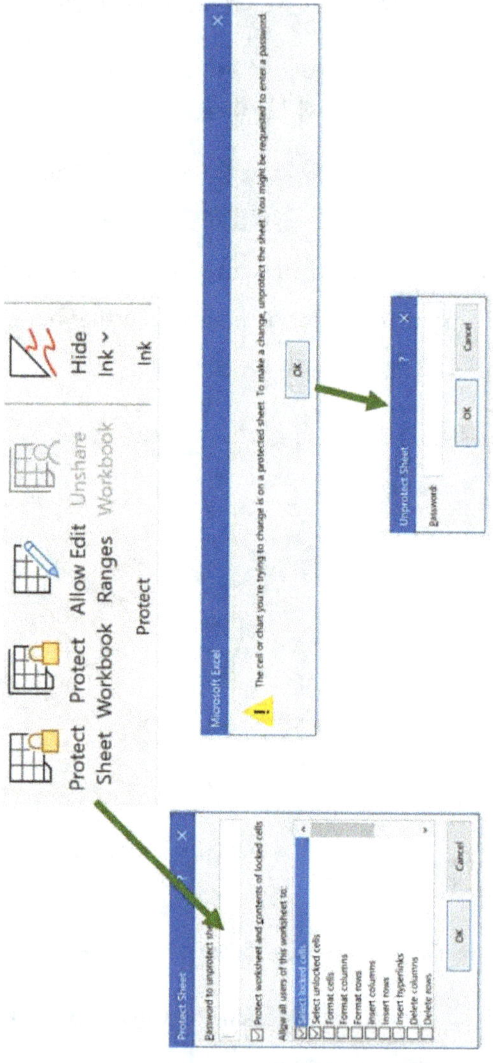

Figure 94: Protect Sheet or Workbook

We will skip the ribbon section "View" in this book, as it is very simple and self-explanatory. Here you can try out different views on your own and thus view the results live and simultaneously. We will now focus on the more advanced and somewhat more complicated ribbon section "Developer".

9 Developer

For this chapter, first make sure that the option "Developer" is activated. The procedure for this can be found in Chapter **1 Excel Interface & important sections.**

9.1 Create Code & Macros

First, we will take a look at the section "Code". In Excel, program codes can be created with "Visual Basic" (Visual Basic is an object-oriented programming language). But don't worry, in this case we don't even have to code ourselves! Excel does that for us when we use the feature "Record Macro". We will see how this works in a moment, but first you have to save your current Excel workbook as "Excel Macro-Enabled Workbook" (see *Fig. 95*; top).

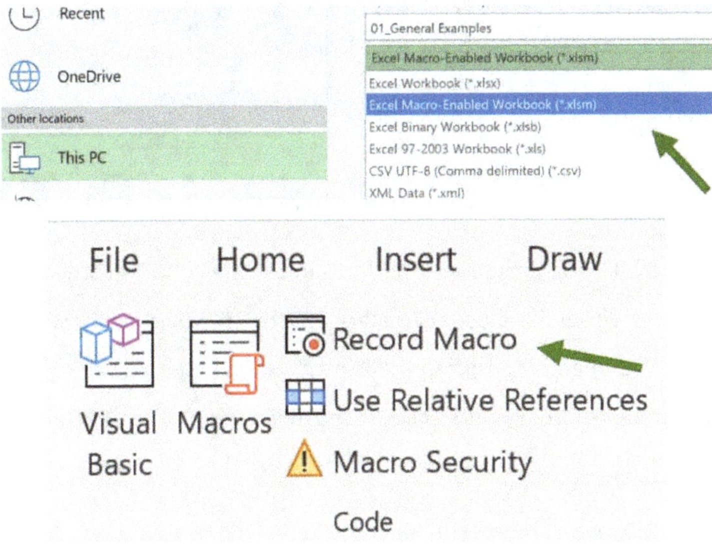

Figure 95: Save workbook (top) & record macro (bottom)

What is a macro anyway? A macro is basically nothing more than a sequence of instructions (code) that can be triggered, for example, simply by clicking a button. In the following, we would like to create such functional buttons with the help of macros for the search function already mentioned in Chapter **7.2 Filter**.

To get started, we would like to create a button that will execute the search. To achieve this, we copy the worksheet created in chapter **7.2** and then click on "Record macro" (*Fig. 95*).

A pop-up window opens in which we can enter a name, a shortcut and – if necessary – a description for the macro (see *Fig. 96*).

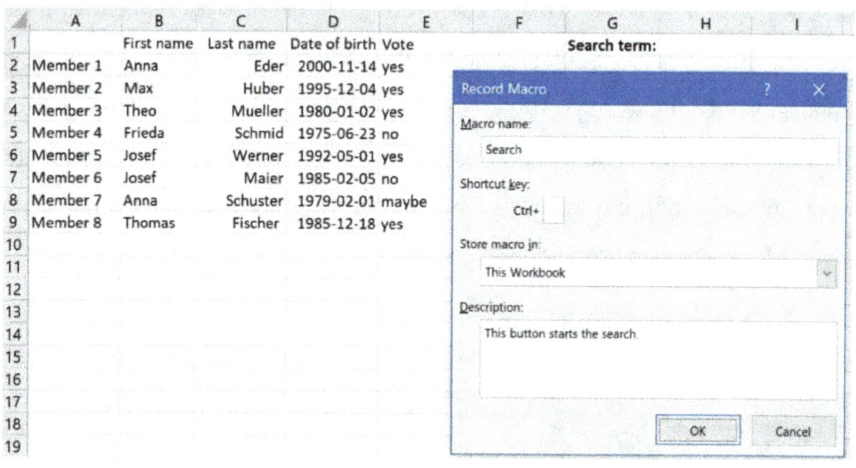

Figure 96: Start "Record Macro"

After clicking "OK", all actions you perform in Excel will be "recorded" and then converted into Visual Basic code. To start the search, you must now click in cell "H1" (search field) and then press the "Enter" key on your keyboard once. Then you can stop the recording with a click in the menu bar (see *Fig. 97*).

Figure 97: Stop recording the macro

This way, you only have to show Excel what you want to get coded using your mouse & keyboard. That is truly genius!

After you have stopped the recording, nothing visually will happen. Therefore, you must now assign this recorded macro to a button. This is done by inserting a control button (*Fig. 98*; step 1) from the menu bar ("Insert"). Do this by dragging a field as shown in *Fig. 98* (step 2), while holding down the left mouse button.

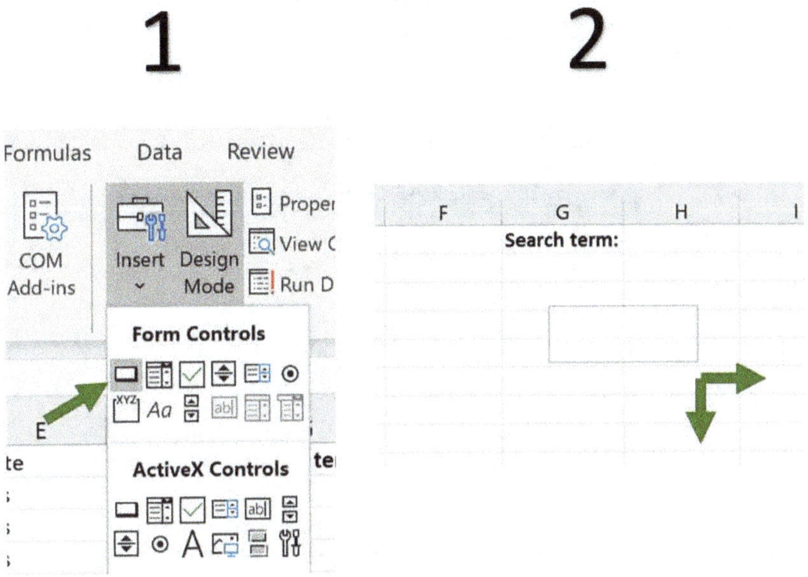

Figure 98: Creating a button for the macro

When you release the mouse button, a pop-up window called "Assign Macro" opens (*Fig. 99*; step 1). Here you can select the previously created macro "Search" and confirm. The search can now be started by entering a search term and clicking on the button "Search" (*Fig. 99*; step 2). You can edit the button by right-clicking on it. If necessary, change the size and enter a suitable name. If an error message is displayed, you must ensure that your macros are enabled (see *Fig. 100*).

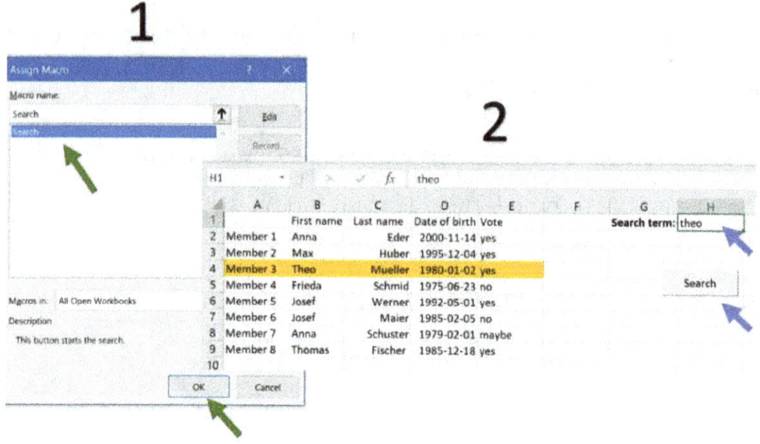

Figure 99: "Assign Macro" and test the search

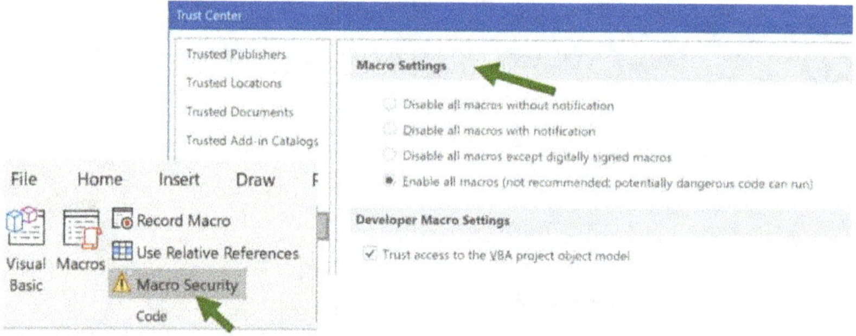

Figure 100: Change "Macro Security" settings in case of an error message

If this does not solve the problem, you can also right-click on the "Search" button and select "Assign Macro" to reassign the macro. Then it really should work without error message.

By right-clicking on the search button and then selecting "View Code" in the section "Controls" (see *Fig. 101*), you open the Visual Basic Editor. Here you can view the code of the macro and modify it if necessary. The code in our example is not very long and actually consists of the statement: **Range("H2").Select**.

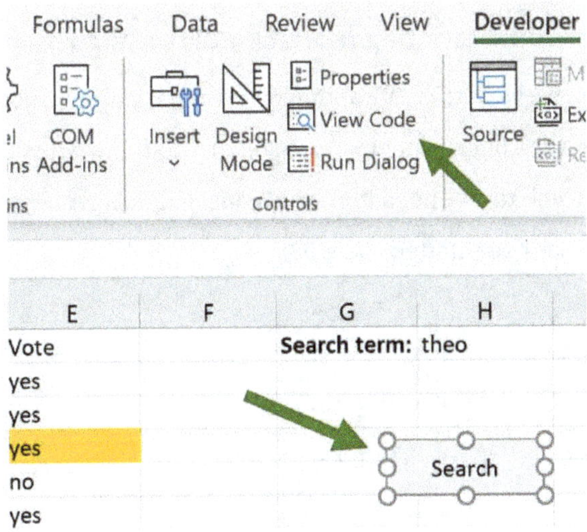

Figure 101: "View Code" of the macro

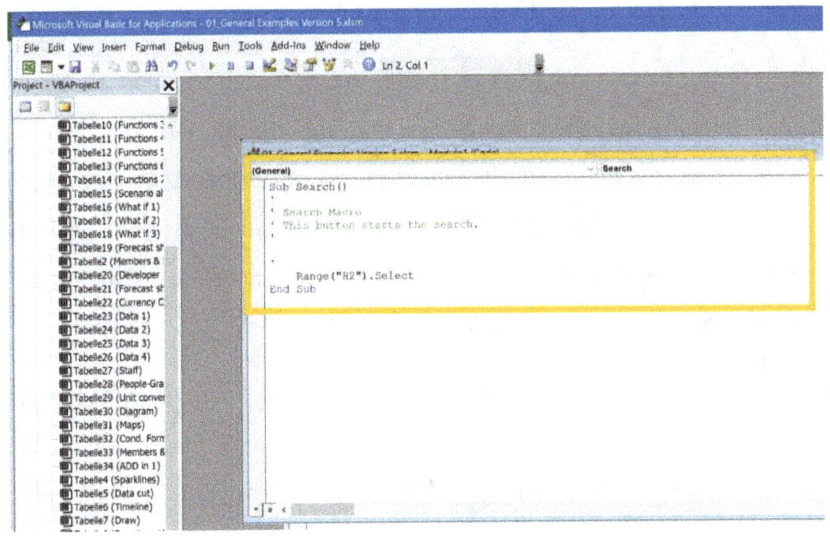

Figure 102: Visual Basic Editor with program code of the macro

The "syntax" of the code is structured as follows (*Fig. 102*): "**Sub**" describes the beginning. The following "**Search ()**" is the name we have assigned. All that is written in green are **comments** and serve to describe the function (also assigned by us). Then follows the command and finally "**End Sub**" as an end-mark.

9.2 Creating more complex Macros

In the next step, we want to create another macro that will only show us the search results, i.e., start the filter "Filter by cell color". To do this, start with the following conditions: a search term – no matter which one, if it delivers a result – is entered and the search has been started (*Fig. 103*).

	A	B	C	D	E	F	G	H
1		First name	Last name	Date of birth	Vote		**Search term:** theo	
2	Member 1	Anna	Eder	2000-11-14	yes			
3	Member 2	Max	Huber	1995-12-04	yes			
4	Member 3	Theo	Mueller	1980-01-02	yes			
5	Member 4	Frieda	Schmid	1975-06-23	no		Search	
6	Member 5	Josef	Werner	1992-05-01	yes			
7	Member 6	Josef	Maier	1985-02-05	no			
8	Member 7	Anna	Schuster	1979-02-01	maybe			
9	Member 8	Thomas	Fischer	1985-12-18	yes			

Figure 103: Initial situation for the macro "Show search results only"

Then start "Record macro" once again and select "Filter by Cell Color" as shown in *Fig. 104*. This way, we have "taught" Excel that we want to use this macro to only display the results of the search. Stop the recording. All further steps are analogous to the previous macro "Search". Finally, create a button and assign the macro. If you have done everything correctly, you can now start the search and then activate the button "Show search results only".

As shown in *Fig. 105*, only the search results are now displayed. To delete the filter, you have to proceed manually (red arrow). This is just perfect for another button, which you could call "Reset search". Try this completely on your own! You will find the codes for the last two buttons as a sample solution, following the *Figures 104* and *105*. The approach for creating is similar to the one described above.

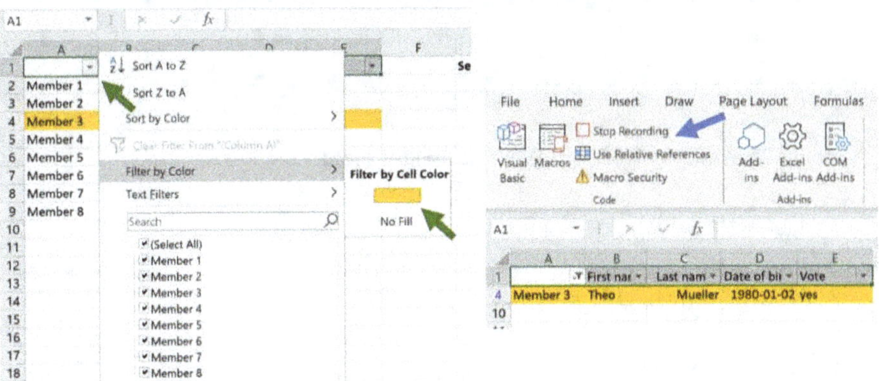

Figure 104: "Filter by cell color" (left side) and "Stop recording" (right side)

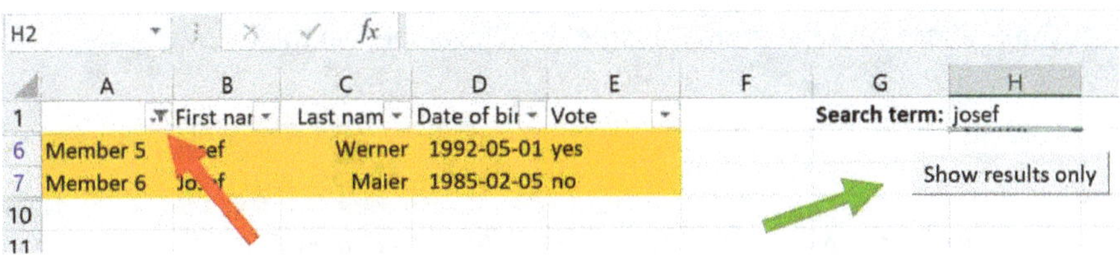

Figure 105: Button "Show results only"

Code for button "Show results only":

Sub Show_results_only()

' Show_results_only macro '

' With a click on this button, only the search results are displayed '

ActiveSheet.Range("$A$1:$E$9").AutoFilter Field:=1, Criteria1:=RGB(255, 192, 0), Operator:=xlFilterCellColor

End Sub

Code for button "Reset search":

Sub Reset_search()

' Reset_search macro '

' A click on this button resets the search, i.e., the color filter is removed and the entry in the search cell is deleted. '

```
ActiveSheet.Range("$A$1:$E$9").AutoFilter Field:=1

Range("H1").Select

ActiveCell.FormulaR1C1 = ""

Range("H2").Select
```

End Sub

Let's take a look at some more functions of "Developer" in the following.

9.3 Add-Ins: "Data Analysis" & "Solver"

In the section "Add-Ins" you can manage your Add-Ins (*Fig. 106*; blue arrow) or load new ones from the store (green arrow).

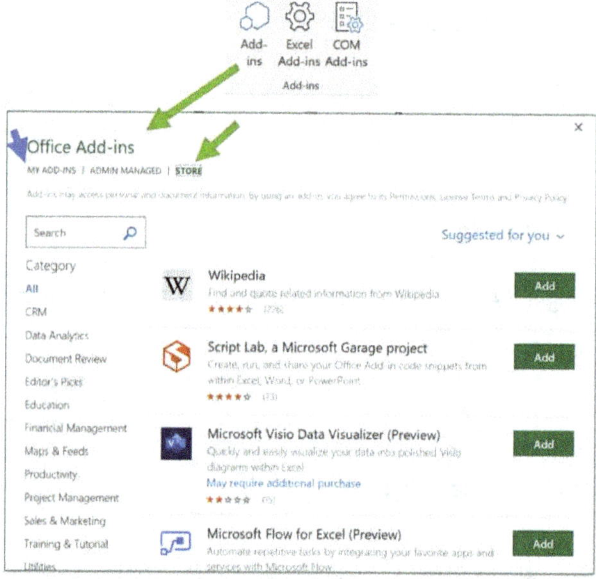

Figure 106: Search Microsoft Store for Add-Ins

You can also activate or deactivate further "Excel Add-Ins" and "COM Add-Ins" (see *Fig. 107*). "Component Object Model (COM) Add-Ins are – in simple terms – ready-made macros that can be used for further automation and offer functions such as "PowerMap" or "PowerPivot". "Power Map", for example, offers the possibility to visualize data in a 3D map (similar to the 2D map from the example in **3.3 Charts**).

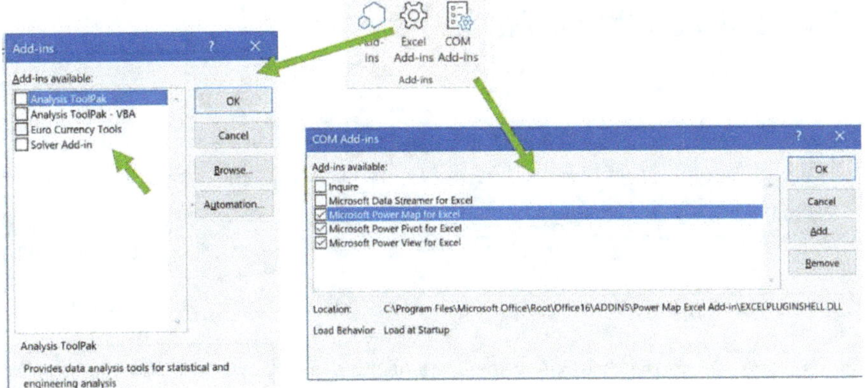

Figure 107: Excel Add-Ins and COM-Add-Ins

In the following, I would like to introduce two more Add-ins: "Data Analysis" and "Solver". First activate the boxes "Analysis ToolPak" and "Solver Add-in" (*Fig. 107*; left side).

The activated functions will show up in the ribbon menu "Data" in the right-hand section (see *Fig. 108*).

With "Data Analysis" you can – for example – perform an Anova analysis, Fourier analysis or a sample test. We will not go into these terms further, as they are relatively complex mathematical concepts. However, if these terms do ring a bell, it will be helpful to know that you can perform these analyses to a certain extent in Excel with this tool.

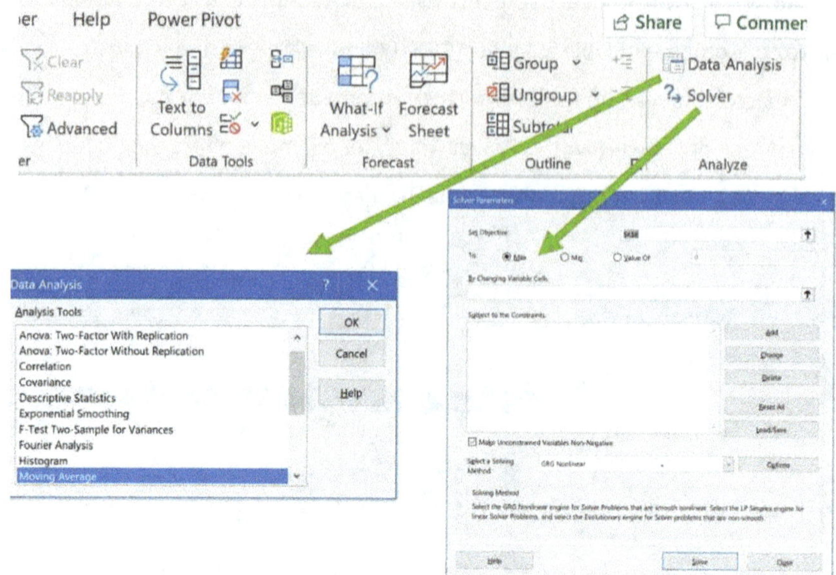

Figure 108: Add-Ins "Data Analysis" and "Solver"

Instead, let's take a closer look at the feature "Solver", as it can be extremely useful when it comes to combination solving. Similar to "Goal Seek" from Chapter **7 Data**, Excel can help you find a target value by varying parameters with conditions set. In concrete terms, this means the following: Imagine you want to rent cars, transporters and minivans for an upcoming move. Of course, you would like to get the cheapest price and all the people in the vehicles. A selection of cars is available in tabular form (see *Fig. 109*).

Note: When calculating total cost (cell D11) and total number of persons (cell C11), it is best to use the functions: **=SUMPRODUCT(A4:A10;C4:C10)**
=SUMPRODUCT(A4:A10;D4:D10)

This function multiplies the rows A4 and C4, A5 and C5, and so on, and sums the entire "package", that means: (A4*C4)+(A5*C5)+...

Then start the Add-in "Solver".

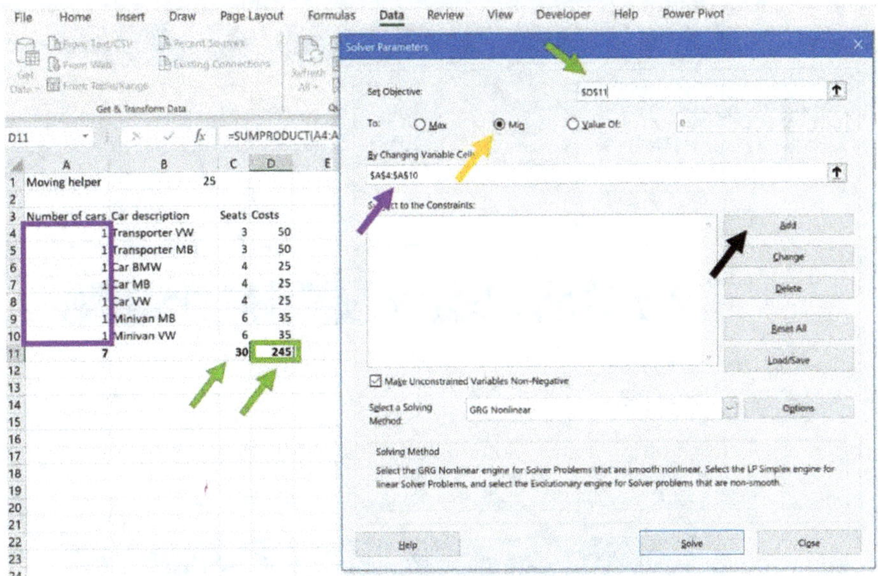

Figure 109: Set "Solver Parameters" to reach target value

Next, select the "Set Objective". In this case, cell D11 ($D$11; total costs; green arrow) and "Min" (orange arrow), since we want to keep this value at a minimum. The cells that Excel should alter are marked in purple (vehicle quantities). Then we have to add three more conditions (**black arrow**).

Set the **first condition** as shown in Figure *110*, step 1. In "By Changing Variable Cells" select the range **$A$4:$A$10**, i.e., the vehicle quantity cells. They should be integer (int = integer = whole number; you can only rent one or two cars but not 1 ½).

The **second condition** (*Fig. 104*, step 2) is: Number of cars should be greater than or equal to 0, i.e., must not be negative.

And the **third condition** has to be: Total number of seats (cell C11) must be greater than or equal to the number of helpers (cell B1) (see *Figure 104*, step 3).

Figure 110: Add constraints

For the last condition, click on "Ok" (or "Cancel" for an empty field) and you will be returned to the window "Solver Parameters". All conditions should now be listed in the area of the orange arrow (see *Fig. 111*). We can leave the solving method at default: "GRG-Nonlinear" (blue arrow) and then click on "Solve". Excel will calculate values (you can see the calculation steps in the Excel bar at the very bottom). After a few seconds, a solution is found, and a selection window is displayed. Just accept the result for now. Then it will be transferred to your table, and you can check it if necessary. Of course, you can also set further conditions, e.g., that you need at least two "Transporter VW" because they have a large loading space which is important for the move. For that set, the condition **"Number of Transporter VW" >= 2.**

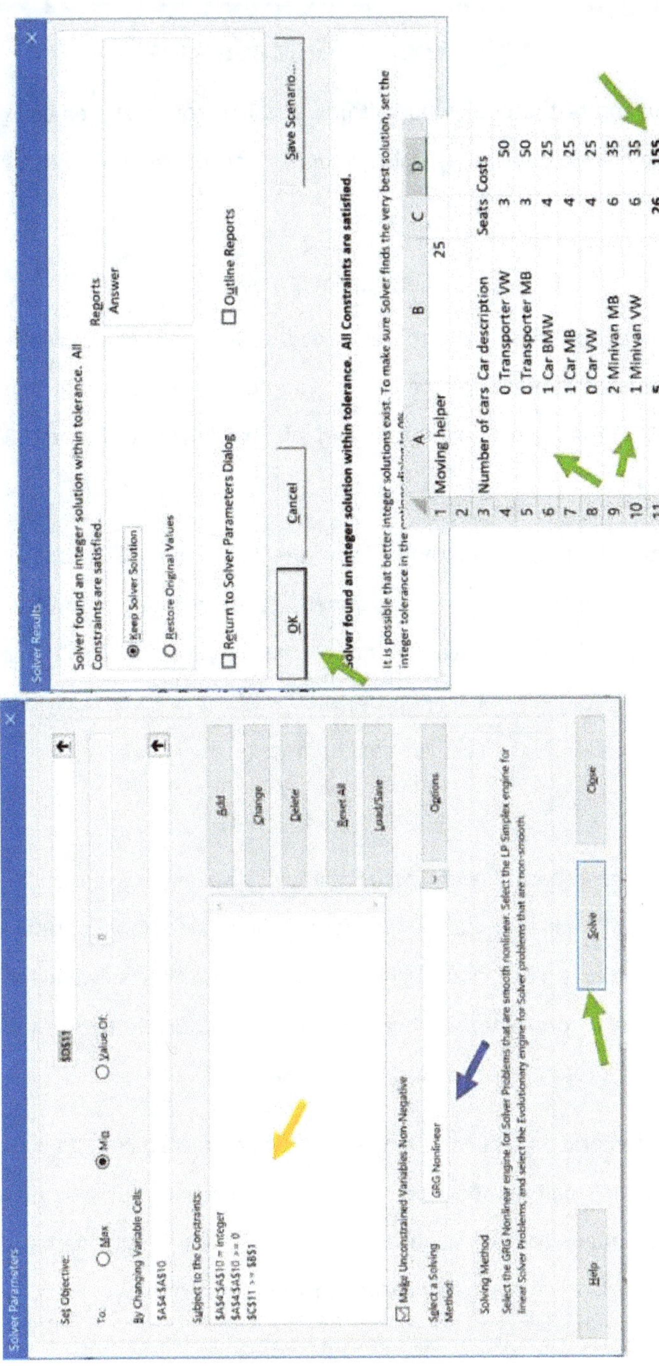

Figure 111: Calculated solution using "Solver"

10 Excel Error Messages

As a conclusion of the book, you will find classic error messages of Excel in this chapter and how to solve them easily. *Remark: For cell format settings, see **Chapter 1.1** Range 4.*

10.1 Error

Understand the problem: With this error code, either the column width of a cell is too small for the contents of the cell, or you have entered a date that is before 01.01.1900. In the format "date", you can only work from the year 1900 in some versions of Excel.

Solve the problem: If the column width is too small, simply drag the column with the mouse to make it larger or, as explained at the beginning of the book, double-click in the space between two columns (alternatively, you can also reduce the font size). If you want to enter a date before 1900, you will unfortunately have to work without the format "date" (use format "number").

10.2 Error #NUM!

Understand the issue: This error occurs if you use a number in a calculation that is too large or too small for Excel (but this is only the case for large or small numbers) or the calculation is mathematically incorrect or at least not solvable for Excel (for example, square root of a negative number). If you divide by the number "0", however, a different error code is displayed (see **10.7**).

Solve the problem: If you simply made a typing error, correct it. If you really have to use large or small numbers or have to calculate with complex numbers (for solving the square root of a negative number), you should perhaps consider another calculation program (e.g., Matlab from Mathworks).

10.3 Error #VALUE!

Understand the problem: If you accidentally perform calculations by referencing to cells that have different or wrong cell formats, this error will be displayed. Example: Addition of a cell formatted as "number" with a cell formatted as "text" (but can still contain a number; the formatting is important). It is also possible that the calculation is simply not performed at all, and you get the calculation formula in the cell as text instead, e.g., "=A1+B2".

Solve the problem: Use identical formatting, such as "number" when calculating numbers, or use the format "standard" (which does <u>not</u> define a specific format).

10.4 Error #NA

Understand the problem: For example, if you use one of the functions VLOOKUP, HLOOKUP or LOOKUP in your spreadsheet, this error may occur. It indicates that a certain value was not found.

Solve the problem: Include the value you are looking for in the range you want to search in, or reference another value. Typically this is just a spelling mistake.

10.5 Error #NULL!

Understand the problem: This error often occurs when a formula is used incorrectly. Typically, a range is not correctly referenced here and therefore cannot be recognized by Excel. Example: =SUM(A1:A10 B1:B10). This specification would lead to the error **#NULL!** because a ";" is missing as a separator element in the range specification. The correct specification is =SUM(A1:A10;B1:B10).

Solve the problem: Search the range of your formula for errors. Often only a ";" or "**(**" or "**)**" is missing.

10.6 Error #NAME?

Understand the problem: The use of text in formulas without quotation marks leads to this error code: "Text". This can also happen if you have a typo in a function, for example =Sun(A1:A10).

Solve the problem: Mark text with " " and check for typos.

10.7 Error #DIV/0!

Understand the problem: Mathematical error, you must not divide by "0".

Solve the problem: Seriously, just do not divide by zero! ;)

10.8 Error #REF!

Understand the problem: Here you have (unconsciously) told Excel to search for something that does not exist in the spreadsheet. This may happen if you refer to a cell from another spreadsheet in a formula, but had previously renamed or deleted it.

Solve the problem: Check the references for spelling, existence, etc.

10.9 Editing locked & Links, Macros without Function

Understand the problem: You cannot edit anything, links, or macros are suddenly without function.

Solve the problem: As a security feature, Excel displays a security warning at startup if external links or macros are detected. If (!?) you trust the links or macros, you have to click on "Enable content", otherwise they will not work. Also check if your file has been saved as an Excel workbook with macros enabled.

10.10 Circular Reference

Understand the problem: A pop-up window appears with the warning of a "circular reference". Circular reference means that a cell refers to itself and thus would cause a circular process. This can happen, for example, if a cell in which you want to have a calculation result **appear, occurs in the calculation itself**, i.e., =TOTAL(**A1**:A10) and you would like to have the **result** displayed **in cell A1**.

Solve the problem: Select another cell to display the result or check whether cells refer to themselves.

10.11 Number becomes Date

Understand the problem: It happens that Excel converts a number into a date.

Solve the problem: In this case, the cell formatting is wrong. The cell was formatted as "date" and therefore displays a date. Select the "standard" or "number" format.

11 Closing Statement

This concludes your Excel training. But after taking a break, it is best for you to start again from the beginning. Sure! Practice the chapters that you found a little bit more difficult step by step so that you really internalize all features and functions. With some practice, the use of Excel will be easier and easier for you from time to time, and you will realize that using Excel's features is a very useful support for your private and professional life.

It was a pleasure for me to (hopefully) help you to understand Excel! My effort was to do this in a simple and compact way. I wanted to give you only the most important and, in my opinion, best features and functions of Microsoft Excel, without confusing you by providing unnecessary information.

Now that you have mastered Excel, inspire your supervisor at work with your knowledge or create astonishing Excel workbooks for your private life or own business!

If you have enjoyed the tutorial, please recommend this book to your colleagues, relatives and friends and/or write a kind review of this book!

Thank you very kindly and all the best for your (Excel) future,

Johannes Wild

Books on topics you might also like

All books are available online on the usual sales platforms. It's best to just search for the title, or feel free to visit my author's page. Some of the books may not be published yet and will be released or found soon. Take a look at the books of your choice and your copy as e-book or paperback!

3D Printing:

CAD, FEM, CAM (3D Object Creation, Design, Simulation):

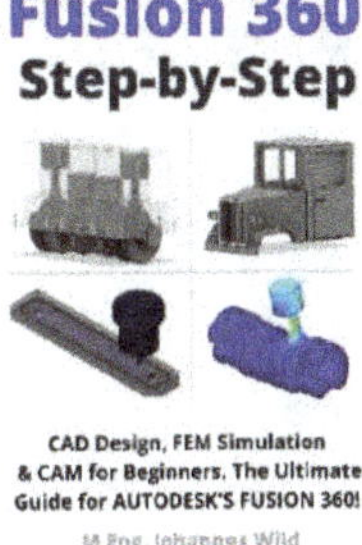

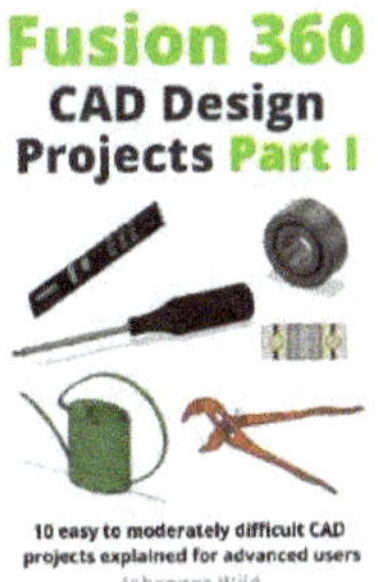

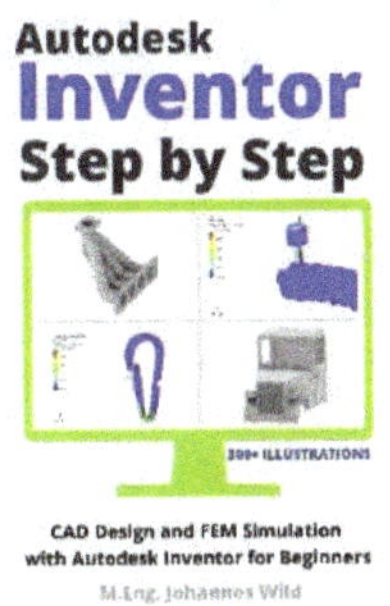

Electrical Engineering:

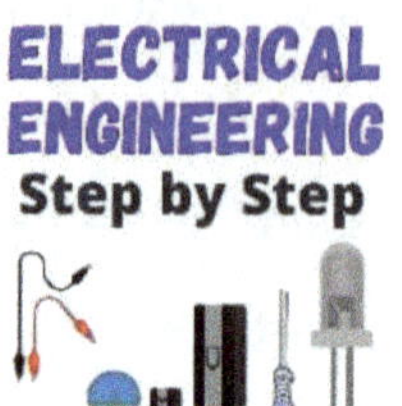

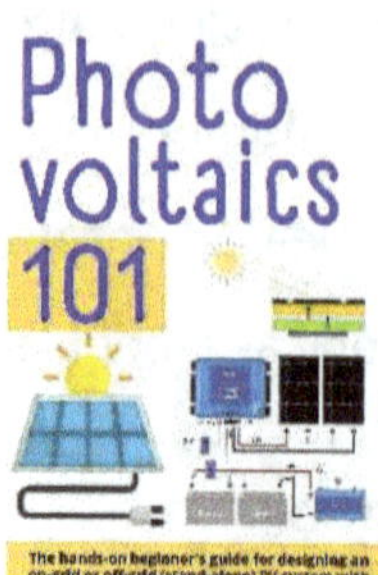
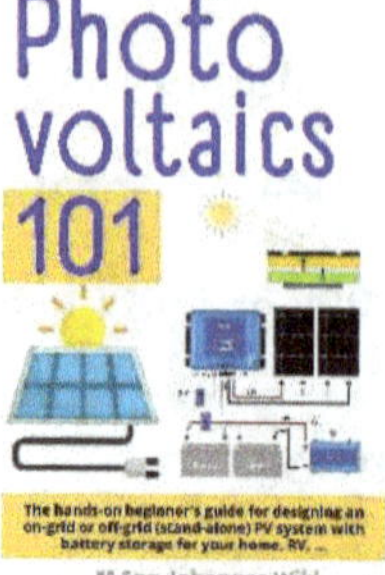

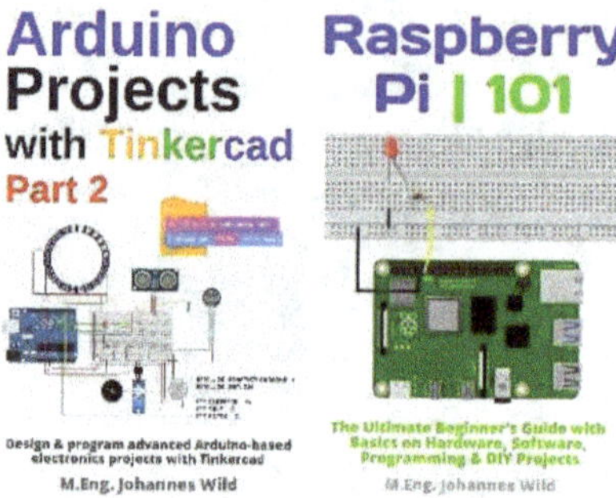

Programming and other Software:

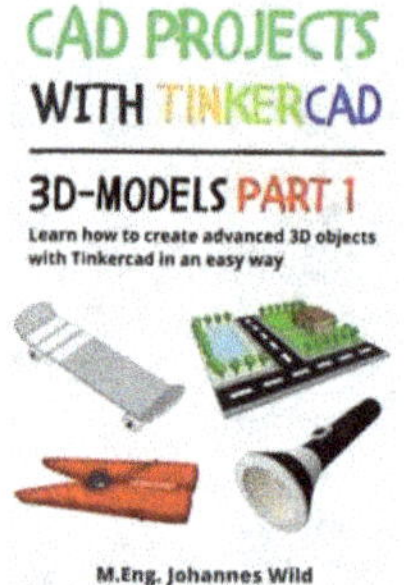

There are also identical video courses for some of these books:

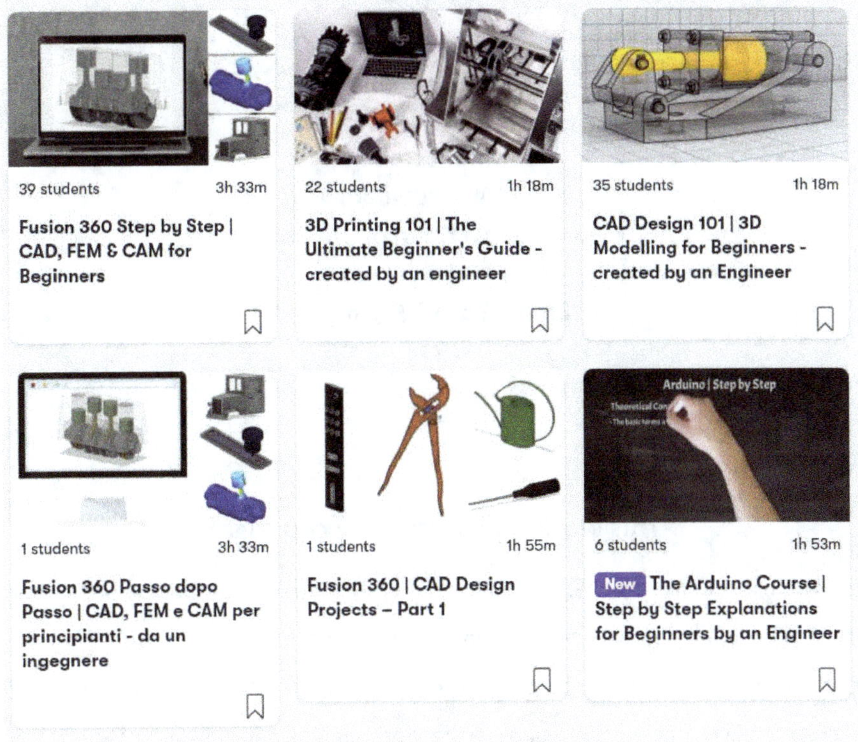

They are hosted on the learning website: skillshare.com

Be sure to use my following friends & family referral link to get a month of membership for free !

(I will get a little bonus if you choose to stay, so we will be both happy. Thanks in advance!)

https://www.skillshare.com/r/profile/Johannes-Wild/854541251

It is best to copy the link in your browser to access the free month !

Sign up today and deepen your knowledge!

Imprint of the author / publisher

© 2023

Johannes Wild
c/o RA Matutis
Berliner Straße 57
14467 Potsdam
Germany

Email: 3dtech@gmx.de

This work is protected by copyright

Thank you so much for choosing this book!